Notes on the Cumbia Family Tree

Collected and Organized

By

Samuel R Whitby,

Author of Exploring the Cumbia Family Tree

Notes on the Cumbia Family Tree

Contents
(with assorted, miscellaneous bits of data interspersed here and there)

Notes on the Cumbia Family Tree

Introduction

The notes that follow are typed copies of handwritten notes that I made while doing research on the Cumbia family tree and history.

The data come from several sources: the family Bible of Oscar and Althea Cumbia; genealogical data from the Internet, County records, archival material from the Library of Virginia, manuscripts at the Virginia Historical Society, and genealogical and anecdotal records from interested individuals and relatives.

In the following, I have tried to identify the data source or sources. A critical reader will be able to make his or her own decisions. about the reliability of any conclusions that were reached.

The data are not presented in the order in which they were taken; rather, they are grouped loosely by county and according to time. Mecklenburg County data, for example, are grouped with other data from that county. With very few exceptions, the notes cover individuals who lived in Virginia. In some cases, the data are just presented, like unconnected pieces of a puzzle, without my knowing exactly where they fit into the larger picture.

When it was possible or logical to present earlier data before later data, I have done so.

The notes concern individuals named Cumby, Cumba, Cumbea, Cumbya, Cumbee, Cumbey, Cumbua, Cumboa, Cumbo, Combea, and Combey, as well as Cumbia. When it has been possible to establish the family relationships, I have done so.

When potentially misleading data are presented, I have sometimes inserted other data or interpretations in brackets []. An example of this is that the father of John H. Cumbia, early in our research, was erroneously identified as James Cumbia. [John Cumbia's death certificate lists George A. Cumbia as his father. Several other documents support that George was John's father. The only James Cumby in Mecklenburg County or Brunswick County was John's brother, James Lewis Cumbea, who was not old enough possibly to have been his father.]

I hope that the notes and the papers based upon the notes will be preserved and made available to other interested individuals. Once upon a time there were real family relationships, the knowledge of which was lost. I do not want that knowledge ever to be lost again.

Notes from the family Bible of Oscar Francis Cumbia, Sr., and Althea Woodall Cumbia-[spellings and punctuation as found]

Oscar Cumbia
August 1, 1914

Marriages-
O.F.Cumbia & Althea Woodall married Aug 4, 1924;
R.A.Cumbia and M.A.Griffith was married December 20-1882;
W.E.Roberts and M.L.Cumbia was married December 14-1904;
R.I.Cumbia and B.E.Dawson was married January 12 -1908;
A.B.Cumbia and G E Lynch was married September 6-1908;
C.A Cumbia and H.D.Hightower was married July.24-1910;
D.D.Cumbia & W H Michael married Dec.27-1916;
G.B.Cumbia, & Bertha Holton married Dec 27 1916;
O.A.Cumbia & J (Illegible) Dawson married Apr. 18 1915;
Married Feb 20, 1918David Cumbia and R.L Harrison ;
Randall Brooks Whitby wed Rosa Rodessa Powell on 13 June [19]71;
Samuel Ray Whitby wed Frances Thorpe Gorman on 5 May 1978[the correct date is May 6];
[Samuel Whitby married Uta McCollum on Sept. 12, 1981];
Noel Cumbia wed Janice Jones in [about]1978;
Robert "Whimpy" Hutcherson Wells wed Juanita (no MI) Whitby;
Emmitt Ray Whitby wed Melynda Gray Barnette on Sept. 27,1992; .

Births- Identifications, in brackets, seem to be in Althea Cumbia's handwriting.
R.A.[Robert Allen] Cumbia born. March 20-1857.
M.A. [Mary Allen] Griffith born. Oct 16-1857.

M.L [Mamie] Cumbia born Nov.-9-1883.
C.A. [Charlie] Cumbia born March.-1-1885.
A.B. [Anna Bell Sue] Cumbia born .Oct 23-1886.
R.I. [Robert Ivan] Cumbia born. Nov.-1-1885.
D D. [Dessie] Cumbia born .Nov. 16-1891.
O.A. [Otis] Cumbia born . Dec.-6-1893.
G.B. [Burnice] Cumbia born Aug-1-1895.
C.D. [David] Cumbia born Sept -9-1899.
O.F [Oscar] Cumbia born. Jan.15-1902;
Randall Brooks Whitby was born on Aug.28, 1952;
Rodessa Whitby was born on 13 Dec 1951;
Colleen Thorpe Gorman Whitby was born on Oct 2, [19]79;
Christopher Eric Cumbia [born]15 Nov [19]82;
David Ray Whitby was born on 15 Nov 1985;
Emily Gray Whitby born 11 Jan [19]94

Deaths-[semi-colons were added for clarity in transcription]
Hattie D. H Cumbia died May 1 1926;
Charlie A. Cumbia died March 20, 1928;
Mary Allen Cumbia died Sept. 28, 1933;
Robert Allen Cumbia died March 8, 1935;
C David Cumbia died Nov. 2, 1939;
Bessie Dawson Cumbia [died] June 15, 1944;
Richlee Harrison Cumbia, died May 28, 1935;
A.B. (Sue) Cumbia Lynch Dawson died Sept 3, 1958
Bertha Holton Cumbia died Feb. 27, 1963;
Otis Allen Cumbia died Feb. 11, 1967;
Josie D. Cumbia died Dec. 27, 1972;
Dessie C. Michael died Aug 4, 1974;
Naomi Cumbia King died March 26 1990 Born Aug 1928;
Robert Ivan Cumbia Sr died August 24, 1972;
Mary Cumbia Ward died Feb 11-1971-born Dec 1930;
Abbbit W. Michael died March 28, 1972 born May 12-1919.
Deaths, continued, separate, adjacent page,-
Mamie C Roberts died June 1970;

Thomas Jefferson Cumbia died Jan 15, 1976;
Herbert W. Cumbia died April 18, 1976;
Hortense C. Parker died Feb. 15, 1976;
O. Douglas Cumbia Born June 29, 1915 died Aug 16, 1986;
Joseph (Joe) Cumbia died July 25 1987;
Christopher Cumbia died July, 1991.

The following was found printed on the back of a sheet of
paper that listed Griffith family information:
The Ages of my People
Mother Father Sisters Brothers [seems to refer to Griffiths]

Bob Cumbia
Brother
Jim Cumbia & wife Emily Crow
Son John Cumbia married Chester Conner
Daughter
John and Chester Cumbias
Son named Lewis Cumbia
William (Willie) Cumbia (Brother of Robert A. Cumbia)
Wife Mattie, Children Winfred, Marvan, Norfleet.
[The above identifies Robert's brothers as Jim and Willie.
The William listed above was Robert's nephew, the son of
Robert's brother, John Henry. Robert did have a brother
named Willie, but he is a different person from the father of
the above 3 children.]

My parents found **four old portrait photographs**, of one
male and three females, in the attic of the Robert Allen
Cumbia home place. Only one of the photos had something
written on the back. One had Louisa written in pencil on the
back, so one can reasonably guess that the photo is of
Robert's sister, Louisa. It seems likely that Robert Allen
would have kept photos of his father, his mother, and his step
mother. Other guesses are that the male was one of Robert's

brothers, Jim. The man in the photograph is neither John Henry nor Robert Allen. The females have been speculated to perhaps be Martha Tucker Cumba, Thomas's wife, or Ann Cabaniss. Someone guessed that they might be Mary and Harriett Early Wells, but they do not seem to be the same people depicted in *The Wellses of Mecklenburg County, Virginia*. The best guess, therefore, seems to be that the people are George, Pamelia, Lucy, and Louisa. The oldest of the ladies is guessed to be Robert's mother, and the younger was probably his step mother.

One sees in George Cumbia's photograph a man with a very hard expression on his face, something consistent with his background as a farmer/overseer, an illiterate man who has experienced the deaths of numerous relatives, including a wife and two children, who has lost his farm in a lawsuit, and who has known the defeat of his state and country in a great Civil War.

Campbell County Notes

Index to Marriage Registers, Campbell County, VA, found on microfilm at the Library of Virginia-reported by date, name, and page number on the marriage register-

Males

1799-Peter Cumby-Book 1, p.37, married Nancy Farthing on November 25, her father was William Farthing,
1800-Emanuel Cumby, 1, p.37, married Molly Farthing on Dec. 27, father was William Farthing,
1807-Charles Cumbee, 1, p.37, married Nancy Leeson on Jan. 20,
1817-Morgan Cumby, 1, p.37, married Leavy [perhaps Lucy, very illegible] Tanner on Nov. 4,
1853-James Cumby, Book 2, p.19,
1855-Peter W. Cumby, 2, p.29,
1857-William S. Cumby, 2, p. 38,
1884-L.C. Cumby,2, p.75.
1899-Benjamin Cumby, Book 3, p. 25,
1906-Radford Cumbie, 3, p. 49,
1910-John Wm Cumby, 3, p.68,
1911-Volney E. Cumby3, p.71,
1912-Cleveland Cumby, 3,p. 74,
1927-Lacy J. Cumby, 3, p. 139.

Females

1808-Margaret Cumbie, to John Powell on June 4, her father was Thomas Cumbee, Book 1, p. 129, Obadiah Edge was minister,
1821-Kitty Cumby, 1, p. 20, married Ezekiel Brooks on Sept. 6, Reuben Rucker was minister,

1821-Rebecca Cumby, mother was Susana Cumby, married Wm. Trent, 1, p. 161,

1823-Sarah Cumby, father was Peter Cumby, married John Trent, Book 1, p. 161,

1825-Susanna Cumby, father was Emmanuel Cumby, married Jesse Purdue on Nov. 21,

1833-Nancy Cumbee-Book 1, p. 58, married Peter Fore on Jan. 29,

1846-Catharine Cumby, father was Samson [perhaps Simson] Cumby, 1, p. 16, married Sampkin Brooks on Sept. 2,

1856-Lucy Ann Cumby, Book 2, p. 34,

Continuation of Index to Marriage Registers, Campbell County, VA

1874-Mollie C., Book 2, p. 175,
1876-Eliza Ann C., 2, p. 63,
1880-Mary Cumby, 2, p. 70,
1886-Alice B. Cumbie, 2, p. 78,
1891-Lelia Cumby, 2, p. 183,
1912-Lula E. Cumby, 3, p. 75,
1920-Gracie Cumbie, 3, p. 109,
1920-Maggie M. Cumbie, 3, p. 11.

Early Census records of Cumbo/Cumbys-

1782 Census of Halifax County lists Thomas Cumbo, with 12 white souls, Charles Cumbo, 7 white souls,

1782 Census of City of Williamsburg lists Edith Cumbo with 2 white souls,

1785 Census of Halifax County lists Thomas Cumbo with 13 white souls, likely to have been Thomas, Sr.,

1785 Census of New Kent County lists Turner Cumbo with 3 white souls,

1810 Census of Charlotte County lists Thomas Cumbs [looks like Cumbo], which may be George Cumby's father.

Campbell County, Marriage Book 2-

1853-James Cumby, p. 19, married Mary Stanley on March 31,
1855-p. 29, Peter W. Cumby , 37, married Saludy N. Cary, he was 37, son of Peter and Nancy Cumby, she was 30, daughter of Richard and Rebecca Cary.

Some early censuses-

1810 Census of Campbell County lists Peter and Emmanuel Cumby,
1820 Census of Charlotte County lists Thomas and Simeon Chumley [Cumby],
1830 Census of Lunenburg County lists Thomas Cumby, with 1 male between 1 and 5, 1 male between 10 and 15 [Major Weatherford], 3 males between 15 and 20 [one of whom was George], 1 male between 50 and 60 [Thomas], 1 female between 1 and 5 [probably Catharine], 1 female between 50 and 60 [probably Agnes].

Located by **General Index to Will Books 1782-1947, Campbell County-**
Book 4, p. 39 refers to the estate of Thomas Cumby, deceased, December 8, 1817, lists his personal property, valued at $39.38, refers to his wife, Mrs. Susannah Cumby. "Cumby's inventory
Agreeable to an Order from the worshipfull Court of Campbell at July Court 1817, after having been first duly Sworn, have appraised, and Inventoried the personal Inventory & Estate of Thomas Cumby Decd as follows, to wit,
One horse and [illegible, perhaps bridle] - $30.00;

Three shocks wheat, and a loose parcel supposed to be 19
Bushels- $28.50;
One feather bed and furniture- $21.00;
One walnut table - $2.50 (stained area);
1 pewter dish and bason, 4 Tin Cups, ½ dozen plates - $2.63;
1 oven and lid and 1 pr hooks -$ 2.00;
1 walnut chest (Bond) - $1.35;
1 Loom, 1 Cotton Wheel - $4.00;
3 hilling hoes, 6 barrells- $4.07;
1 pair Iron Traces, Clovis pin and Singletree- $3.00;
1 water pail, 1 churn- $0.83;
1 pair Cotton Cards and 1 pepper box- $1.00;
2 plowhoes and 1Coalter- $2.25.
Given under our hands this 18th day July 1817
Benjamin Tanner
Nathan Tanner
Samuel Martin

An email sent to interested family members:

"Here lately I have been too busy to drive to the LVA and do as much research as I have wanted to do. Trying to make use of the little time that has been available, I have studied my notes and tried to find some of the meanings hidden among the data. This morning I will mention some deductions made from the notes, regarding the siblings of Thomas Cumby.

For several reasons I believe that the father of "our" Thomas Cumby was Thomas Cumbo/Cumby, Sr., of Halifax then Charlotte then Campbell County. George Cumby's father married in Halifax County. At the time his name was spelled - phonetically, no doubt, for Thomas signed his x - as Cumboa or Cumby. His son Major Weatherford was born in Charlotte County. George was born in Campbell County. Thomas Cumbo/Cumby,

Sr., sold land in Halifax, moved to Charlotte, then moved to Campbell, where he died in 1817. His wife in several documents is identified as Susannah (or Susanner).

In 1782 and 1785 Thomas, Sr., lived in Halifax County. In 1785 his family was composed of "13 white souls." This leads one to wonder who were the ten siblings of George and Major's father. My notes give some good indications and some fine guesses. First, I will mention the documented relationships. In 1790 Molly Cumbo married James Mathews.In 1804 Major Cumbie married Margaret Mical [perhaps should be Michael]. In 1806 Patsy Cumbee married Elisha Smith. In 1808 Margaret Cumbee married John Powell. In 1821 Rebekkah Cumby married William Trent. All of the preceding specifically identify Thomas or Susannah or both as parent(s). Thomas Cumboa married Agnes Weatherford (also spelled Wetherford) in Halifax County, but Thomas's parents, at least in the data I have found so far, are not identified. One may, I believe, reasonably guess that, given that the older Thomas was identified elsewhere as Senior, that Thomas was a son of Thomas and Susannah. Other data found later may prove me wrong, but that is the way it seems at this time. In notes that are not before me now, in other words in my failing memory, there is a record of Daniel Cumby's being the son of Thomas. Undocumented but probable are the cases of Patience, Peter, and Emmanuel. Patience Cumbow married Robert Wilson in 1787. Peter married Milly Ramsey in Halifax County in 1785. I believe he was the same Peter who married, most likely as a widower, Nancy Farthing in Campbell County in 1799. Charles Cumbee married Nancy Leeson in Campbell County in 1806, and Emmanuel Cumby married Nancy Farthing's sister, Molly, in 1800 in Campbell. Mary Cumbo married Evan Young in 1792 in Halifax County. Sarah Cumbo married Ezekiel Mathews in 1793.

My proposed list of siblings includes the following: Molly, Major, Patsy, Margaret, Rebekkah, Patience, Mary, Sarah, Thomas, Daniel, Peter, Emmanuel, and Charles. An observant reader will note that this makes 13 siblings. I believe that Peter and (perhaps) Charles were out on their own by the time the 1785 Census was taken, and assuming that to be true would reconcile the list of siblings with the '13 white souls.' "

1857-p. 38,William S. Cumby, 23, son of Simeon and Emma Cumby, married Sarah Strong, 25, daughter of Thomas and Margaret Strong, married by Tho. E. Locke,

Bureau of Vital Statistics, Campbell County, from microfilm at the Library of Virginia-
Deaths, 1857, p. 31, line 15, Nancy Cumby died on Nov. 1, from old age (59), parents were Wm. & Nancy Farthing, info provided by Thos Cumby, son.
The Campbell County Death Register gives the above information with the difference that the age of Nancy Farthing Cumby was given as 89.

Campbell County Order Book 23-
"A deed of bargain and sale from John Reid to Agness Cumby, Jemima Cumby and Robert R. Cumby together with the certificates of acknowledgement and relinquishment of donor"..." endorsed, presented in court, ordered to be recorded"

From **Thomas Robinsons's Tax Book of 1810-**
Peter Cumbee and Emmanuel Cumbee paid tax on 195 acres of land.

Oct. 4, 1869, **Book 35**, p. 98, Agness and Jemima Cumby paid $33.75 to Jno. W. Elam for 25 acres.

Book 31, p. 531-
Peter Cumby sold Agness 45 acres for $180, July 12, 1859.

Peter Cumby sold Peter W. Cumby 45 acres for $5.
"This Indenture made this 19th day of November 1839 between Peter Cumby of the one part and Peter W. Cumby of the other part all of the County of Campbell and the State of Virginia witnesseth that the said Peter Cumby for & in consideration of the natural love and affection which he has and bears for his said son, Peter W. Cumby"… "45 acres patented to William Farthing $5"
Peter Cumby X his mark

1850 Census of Campbell County, VA
Fam., Dwell. #
1023- James Cumby, 22, Laborer;
1104-Simeon Cumby, 47, Miller;
"   -Aimy Cumby, 50;
"   -Mary   "   ,28;
"   -Thomas "   ,23;
"   -Martha "   ,21;
"   -Sarah   "   ,19;
"   -William "   ,16;
"   -Narcesses " ,13.
1850 Census of Campbell County, VA
1229-Thomas Cumby ,40, farmer,
"   -Eliza   "   , 35,
"   -Sonia A. "   , 19 (name is illegible),
"   -William W. "   , 17, farmer,
"   -Frank R.   "   , 16,
"   -John   "   , 14,

"   -Elizabeth   "   , 12,
"   -Martha   "   , 10,
"   -Thomas   "   , 7,
"   -Peter   "   , 4,
"   -Francis   "   , 1
1230-Peter Cumby ,   85, farmer
"   -Nancy   "   ,   80,
"   -Peter   "   ,   30, farmer,
"   -Robert   ,   25, farmer,
"   -Agnes   ,   42,
"   -Jemima   ,   40

1860 Census of Campbell County-
Fam.916, Dwel.930-

Peter Cumby-	100-day laborer
Robert W. Cumby-	39-rough carpenter
Peter Cumby-	44-laborer

Fam.917,Dwel.931-

Aggie Cumbey-	57-wife and farmer
Jemima Cumbey-	41-domestic
Nancy S. " -	33
Virginia " -	3
Nancy C. " -	1

From *MARRIAGES OF CAMPBELL COUNTY, VIRGINIA-, 1782-1810*-Powell, John and Margaret Cumbee, bond June 4, 1808. Consent by Margaret and Thomas Cumbee also. John Powell (b.) and Nathan Tanner (b.); Susanner Cumbee (w.), Nancy Cumbee, and Nathan Tanner (w.) M.R. entry [was] made twice by Obadiah Edge, June 5, 1808.

From **Bonds and Consents, Mecklenburg County**, on microfilm at the LVA-
April 12, 1834, George Comby posted a Bond of $150 in order to marry Pamelia Wells. Her father, Henry Wells, gave his written consent. Consent was witnessed by [illegible] Wells, John Gwaltney, [illegible]Comby. The Comby signature looks like it might have been Margaret [Madj W Comby].

Campbell County Chancery Order Book 1831-1850-
October 11, 1849 John B. Weatherford against Drury C. Moorman, Charles I. Oliver, H. Hazelwood- " For satisfactory reasons appearing to the court, it is ordered, that these suits be dismissed."

Mecklenburg County, Virginia-

Bureau of Vital Statistics, Mecklenburg County-

Mary T.Wells, died on August, 1887, from liver disease, at the age of 68, info provided by James L. Cumba, nephew. Parents were given as "unknown."

May 14, 1872, Pamelia A. Cumba was born to James L. Cumba, miller, and Emily F. Cumba, with info provided by Jas. L. Cumba.

Beulah Y. V. Cumba , white female, died in March 1893 at the age of one year and four months, from consumption. She was the daughter of G. A. and D. E. Cumba. G. A. Cumba, father, provided the info.

Geo. A. Combea died on June 10, 1896, from consumption. He was the son of J. L. and E. F. Combea. His wife was Lizzie Combea.

L.L. Cumby, 17, married Robert D. Lucy, 23, on January 23, 1884. She was the daughter of J.H. and W. Cumby.

June 1870 - twin children of George and Lucy Morgan died, cause of death was unknown, lived one day. Info was provided by P. Cumby, grandmother [Martha Cumby, Patsy].

November 2, 1873 – Louisa Cumbia died, cause of death was consumption. This entry looks like "Laura ", but her parents were listed as George and Pamelia. Maybe Laura was Laura Louisa or Louisa Laura.

Ann E. Cumba married Paschal Y. Cabiness on Sept. 15, 1858. He was born in Lunenburg County. His parents were

Asa B. and R. (wife) Cabiness. Her parents were George Cumba and P. A. [,]wife.

Mecklenburg County Register of Marriages, p.179, 1872, line 43- Dec. 19, 1872, G.A. Cumby, 60, married L.M.Tucker, 28. Both were widowed. His place of birth was Campbell County, hers was Mecklenburg County. His parents were "T & A Cumby." Hers were M&M Tucker. [George Cumby's age is lower here than other documents would indicate to be the case. This is a second marriage, after George's marriage to Pamelia Wells.]

Mecklenburg County General Index to Wills and Lists of Heirs-

George A. Cumby-Bk 24, p.571,
George A. Cumby-Bk.24, p.583, [this line and the one preceding it refer to the disposition of the estate of George Cumby]

George Cumbia's estate included the following: 6 chairs, $1.50; cooking utensils, $ 0.50; plow, $4.00; corn, 17 barrells, $42.50; 1 hog, $3.50; 1125 lbs. fodder, $5.62; tobacco, not stripped, $25.37; horse, $15.00; ½ interest in wagon, $12.00; Grub hoes, $1.50; Box and contents, $0. 25; Little bed, $3.00; Gun, $2.00; Bed stead $0.50; Table and contents, $2.00. George Cumbia's estate was valued at $141.26.

On Nov. 21, 1884 the sale of George Cumbia's personal property brought $100. 88. R.A.Cumbia bought 2 barrells of corn for $2.98, 1 horse for $16.00, and 1 hog for $3.72. John H. Cumbia was administrator of estate. From Book 25, p. 21.

R.A.Cumbia-Bk 30 p.31,
Pamelia Cumby-Bk 16 p.427, Will of Henry Wells,
E.F. Cumby –   Bk 26, p. 575,
Mary Cumbia – Bk 28, p. 492,

The Will of Henry Wells (father of Mrs. George Cumby)-
"In the name of God Amen – This 14th day of May one
thousand eight hundred and forty seven~ I Henry Wells of
the County of Mecklenburg and State of Virginia being of
sound mind and disposing memory but of feeble health &
body, well assured of the uncertainty of life & that it is
ordained by our Creator for man once to die, do make and
constitute this as my last Will & Testament, revoking and
dissannsiting [?] all others.

1st I desire all my just & lawful debts of every description
shall be paid as early as practicable after my disease[sic],
after discharging which I devise & bequeath the balance of
my estate in manner follow to with. To the five children of
the intermarriage with my first wife Polly Davis, I give and
bequeath the legacy now in expectancy, left to my said and
first wife by her uncle William Barney. Viz. To William
Wells, John Davis Wells,& to my daughters Sally Taylor
Farley (formerly Wells) Susannah Danson Roberts (
formerly Wells)& MarthaAnn Jane Chandler (formerly
Wells) to whom and their heirs forever, also all the property
of whatsoever description at various times, which I may have
given or advanced them, to them and their heirs forever,
having given off all I intend from my estate and that they
shall in no wise or by any construction of my will have
possess or heirs or ever hereafter receive any benefit from the
balance of my estate after my decease.

2ndly. All of my estate both real and personal which I now
have in my possession or may hereafter acquire I intend for
the sole use and benefit of my beloved wife Mary and her
five children in manner following to wit, to my beloved wife
Mary during her natural life I give and bequeath all my estate
both Real and Personal and my wish and desire is that she

may make any advancement of my property of any description from my estate in her possession to either of her children at any time during their minority or before they arrive at years of discretion which she may think it proper but should she intermarry, after my disease[sic], then and in that even[t]she shall only be entitled to the use of one third of my estate during her life and at her death the whole as heretofore mentioned both Real and personal I give and bequeath to my five children Pamelia Ann Burroms [perhaps Burrows] Cumby (formerly Wells), Mary Taylor Wells, George Henry Wells, Edward Lewis Wells, Harriet Early Wells to be equally divided between them to them and their heirs forever. 3rd My wish and desire after my disease[sic]is that my son Edward Lewis reside with his mother & assist her in the management of the plantation, for which services rendered he shall receive a liberal remuneration.

4th I leave my beloved wife Mary my whole & sole executive to this my last Will & Testament the date and year above written and expect my son Edward Lewis to give such assistance as she may require in the management of my Estate.

Henry Wells   X mark

From **Mecklenburg County Deed Book**-
Re. George Combey's farm, Nov. 17, 1837-"…Tucker's Tract containing by estimate one hundred and a half acres be the same more or less and bounded as followeth by Robert Walker's land by Elizabeth Hulberson Pennington Letts and others and I the said Thos Keeton as agent and aforesaid to warrant and ever defend the right tittle [sic] and interest of the said tract or parcel of land and every part thereof unto the said George Combey his heirs and assigns forever …." Paid $190.95 for land.

Mecklenburg County Deed Book 27, p. 402-Jan. 15, 1838- sale final- "approved and admitted to record."

Robert Allen Cumbia's death certificate identifies George Cumbia as his father, does not identify the mother. Information was provided by his son, R. I. Cumbia, Sr.

Marriage records of Mecklenburg County, microfilm at LVA-

Mary Susana Cumby, 25, married David Gescoyn Brooks, 33, on October 19, 1865. They were married at the house of her father, George Cumby, by H. Arnold. David's parents were John and Elizabeth Brooks. David was born in England. Book 1, p. 24. James L. Cumby married Emily F. Crow on November 30, 1865-Marriage Book 1, p. 25.

Ann E. Cumba married Paschal Y. Cabaniss on September 15, 1858-Book 1. P.11.

Geo. A. Cumba died in September, 1884. Cause of death was "tincture." He was 79 years old, and he was born in Campbell County. Information was provided by R.A. Cumba, son. His mother was not identified, but his father was identified as Thomas Cumba.

Lucy Tucker, wife of George Cumby, died on August 13, 1884. She died from "womb." She was 48 years old. Her parents were Merritt [illegible] and Martha Tucker.

In 1892 A.S.Cumbea, white female daughter of J.L. & E.F.Cumbea died at 19 years of age. She was single. Cause of death was unknown.[The 1880 Census of Lunenburg County lists a five year old daughter named Angelina, evidently the same person as A.S.]

Mecklenburg County marriage books-

Susana Cumby, daughter of Geo. A. and Permelia Cumby, marriage to David Brooks, by H. Arnold Bk., 1 p. 24.
James L. Cumby [to Emily Crow], Bk. 1, 25.
E. Green [to Sallie Tucker], Bk. 1, p. 33.
G.A Cumby [to Lucy Tucker] Bk. 1, p. 43.
R. A. Cumby [to Mary Griffith] Bk. 1, p. 60. James L. Cumby married Emily F. Crow on November 30, 1865-Marriage Book 1, P. 25.

Ann E. Cumba married Paschal Y. Cabaniss on September 15, 1858-Book 1. P.11.

In 1892 A.S.Cumbea, white female daughter of J.L. & E.F.Cumbea died at 19 years of age. She was single. Cause of death was unknown.[The 1880 Census of Lunenburg County lists a five year old daughter named Angelina, evidently the same person as A.S.] James L. Cumby married Emily F. Crow on November 30, 1865-Marriage Book 1, p. 25.

Ann E. Cumba married Paschal Y. Cabaniss on September 15, 1858-Book 1, p. 11.

Mecklenburg County death register-

Geo. A. Cumba died in September, 1884. Cause of death was "tincture." He was 79 years old, and he was born in Campbell County. Information was provided by R.A. Cumba, son. His mother was not identified, but his father was identified as Thomas Cumba.

Lucy Tucker, wife of George Cumby, died on August 13, 1884. She died from "womb." She was 48 years old. Her parents were Merritt[illegible] and Martha Tucker.

D. A. Hudson performed the marriage of R. A. Cumby and M. A. Griffith.

The Will of Sallie Francis Griffith [Mary Griffith's mother] specifies that she must have a gravestone with her name on it.
 Mecklenburg County Will Book 24, p. 571 : " Know all men by these presents, that we Jno H. Cumby, R. A. Cumby, and J. L. Cumby & Paschal Y. Cabaness are held and firmly bound…[for] the sum of $ 250."-refers to the estate of George A. Cumby.

Will Book 24, p. 583, Dec. 15, 1884 Appraisement of estate of George A. Cumbia for $ 141.25, naming John H. Cumbia as Adm. Property was sold for $103.88, dated Nov. 21, 1884. [There must be some sort of error in these dates.]

Mecklenburg Deed Bk 27, p. 402-
George Combey's farm was "bounded as followeth by Robert Walkers land by Elizabeth Hutcherson Pennington Letts and others."

James Cumbae bought out Harriet Wells on November 12, 1892   [Book 51, p. 564] for $ 250, with tax of fifty cents, land in Buckhorn Township.

From THE HUTCHESON FAMILY OF MECKLENBURG COUNTY VIRGINIA, in the Arnold Library at South Hill, VA-

"Charles Sterling Hutcheson, born 1804, died, 1881, Col. In the Militia, Presiding Justice of the County Court, Member of the Legislature and a Trustee of Randolph-Macon College" is buried in Hutcheson-Riddick Family Cemetery, which can be found by taking highway 671 from the telephone tower off 660, look for farm rd. to south (right) on hill after crossing Allen's Creek bridge. Follow bearing to the left. Go through metal fence. Cemetery is west of old home place off farm road, enclosed in stone wall.

Hutcheson was a "friend" and lender to George A. Cumby.

Crowe Family Cemetery – "Located at the Crenshaw farm off Hwy. 660 behind the old house at the end of the road. Look in pasture behind the old house. Many graves marked with field stones." The previous entry came from Cemetery and Tombstone Records of Mecklenburg County Virginia, Vol 2. Emily Crowe is supposed to be buried there, possibly James Cumbea also.

Vol. 1 of the above gives the burial place of James and Walter Cabaniss as Woodland Cemetery in Chase City, VA.

1880 Census of Mecklenburg County: family no. 333-Cumby, George, WM, 55 [which is almost certainly far too young], farmer, cannot read or write; Cumby, Lucy, 31 [perhaps 37]; Cumby, Robert, 21.

Bureau of Vital Statistics, Mecklenburg County, 1862-1896, Reel 26, LVA-
Henry A. Combia [perhaps Combea] died on December 10, 1894 [date is very hard to read]. His father was Geo. A. Combea, farmer, b. in Mecklenburg; mother was JEC Combea

Mecklenburg County General Index to Marriages,
Positive Reel 47 at the LVA-
Alexr. N. Griffis married Sarah F. Coley on May 23, 1855,
Marriage Book 1, p.3. [Sarah Coley is most likely to be Sallie
Coley].

Consent of Henry Wells for his daughter to marry-

"...the clerk of Mecklenburg County is here by orthorized
[to] give License to George Comby to Marry my Daughter
Parmelia A B this shall be your sufficient orthoriety Given
under my hand and seal this 12th day of April 1834   Henry
Wells
Witness
[il, looks like Lisher] Wells
illegible
Il Comby[looks like it might be Margaret.No, This is Madj
W Comby!
John Gwaltney

**Email correspondence between Carolyn Davis and Sam
Whitby-**

"Dear Carolyn,
If you don't mind, I will cut and paste to include your
message among my Cumbia notes. I knew I had seen the
name Chesley Curtis before, but I didn't remember when. I
knew that James Edmondson was a neighbor.
There were other potentially helpful references indexed. One
I would guess has to do with James and Emily Cumbea
selling their land or perhaps mortgaging it. This one was to a

Wells, the first name of whom slips me at the moment. [The name was Warner Wells.] I will have to go back and take careful notes when there is time. Also, a couple of references are to George and Pamelia's deed to Marie Coleman, and those references are dated 1894. I don't understand, since P. died in 1870-72 and Geo. died in 1884, with the property having been sold in 1875. I didn't have time to even look at those. Also, there is a reference to a sale of land by E.G. Cumby in 1877. All in all, I will just have to go back and take my time and try to figure out what those things mean. Regarding Thomas's being in Halifax in 1851, that may mean that he was over-seeing at some plantation there, or it may mean that Thomas and Martha were separated by then. Thank you for your info, which is very helpful as always.
Sam
----- Original Message -----
From: ecarolyn davis
To: Sam Whitby
Sent: Wednesday, July 07, 2004 4:42 PM
Subject: Re: Cumbys

Sam, I was so glad you found this, I had not seen any of it. I would be most grateful to know anything else you found or find. Somehow i never got into the chancery records in the courthouse in Boydton because they were locked upstairs and someone had to take me up there, the clerk of the court would take me but I never happened to catch him there when I had the time to go up there. I am sure there is a treasure there and I still hope to do that in the future.

Some background on the names you mentioned:

Chesley S. Curtis born abt 1805 is the brother to Martha Patsy Curtis. I don't know who the Lett is you mentioned but Chesley S. Curtis married Faithy Hubbard Lett whose father was Hardiway Lett who was a big land owner and rich by the standards of that time. There are numerous Lett/Curtis marriages and it could have been any one of the Letts, I would think there was a family connection to who ever they owed money.

James Watkins Edmondson was a merchant whose mansion and store was across the road from the present day prison camp which made his store across from Martha and Thomas' 100 acres her father gave her while he was still living. The old home was indeed a mansion because I remember it before it was torn down by the WPA. James W. Edmondson is the person who Lucy Ann and Green sold their mother's 100 acres to. And then to make things more confused, James W. Edmondson was the grandson of Sally F. Curtis, also sister to Martha Patsy.

There is an old family story that after losing so much land after the Civil War to pay debts,the Curtis' made a pact among themselves to never let anymore Curtis land get out of the family, if they sold they must sell back to a family member. It appears they did just that. My gr grandfather, Zachariah Curtis, Jr traded 400 acres for an old mule after the war to be able to till some land as all his livestock had been confiscated by the Confederacy for the army use. Just FYI stuff. Carolyn

-------------- Original message --------------
Carolyn,
I went to the LVA today and spent most of my time looking at Halifax County death records. Just before I had to leave I took a glance at a deed index for Mecklenburg County. There were about a dozen entries relevant to Thomas/George/etc., some of which I had never seen. I stole a few minutes to glance at the deeds. One had Thomas putting up his farm,

200 acres, in Lunenburg County in order to pay debts to a merchant. Two interesting names came up in that deal, Lett (I don't remember the first name) and Chesley Curtis. Thomas had to pay off some bonds or Lett and Curtis could sell his farm and property to pay the debt. A list of Thomas's property was an interesting part, and I will send that later. Also, Thomas and Martha sold their interest in the estate of Zach Curtis to James Edmunds (or Edmundson). Thomas was described as a resident of Halifax Co. and Martha as a res. of Mecklenburg. A bad storm is coming, so I will write more later.

Email sent 7/15/2004:

"This morning I looked at some deeds at the Library of Virginia, in which Cumby ancestors were listed as Grantors. In **Deed Book 29, on page 538**, I found an agreement in 1842 by **Thomas Cumbie** [one of the very few times I have found that spelling] with Drury H. Lett et al [Chesley Curtis], a Deed of Trust putting up as collateral Thomas's farm and property in Lunenburg County. The agreement is clearly written but fairly lengthy. It can be summarized by saying that Thomas owed numerous merchants who wanted to be paid. Thomas's property was described as follows: "1 sorrel mare & colt 1 cow. 3 ploughs. 2 coulter ploughs, 4 hill hoes, 4 grub hoes, 1 Loom [illegible] sitting chairs 2 spinning wheels 7 beds & furniture 2 bed steads 2 tables 1 Doz Table Knives & forks 2 dishes 2 pitchers, 1 doz: plates, 2 ovens 2 pots 1 Coffee pot 1 spider [?] 1 set cups and saucers[and] a certain tract or parcel of land lying and being in the County of Lunenburg [200 acres, 150 acres life estate and 50 acres fee simple, whatever that means]." The deal basically was that Thomas would pay up or his property would be sold. I have not seen for sure how this turned out, but I can guess.

Book 41, page 575, records the sale in 1877 by E.G. [Green] Cumby of his interest in Martha C. Curtis's 100 acres, for $25 to W.C.Curtis and James Edmonson. It describes Martha's property as "bounded in the North by Estate of Z. Curtis & W.C. Curtis, on the East by Giles Bowens' Est., on the South by Stony Cross road, and on the west by J.W.Edmonson's Est."

Book 51, page 565 records a Deed of Trust by which James and Emily Cumbea bought 154 acres from Harriett Early Wells for $250. Warner Wells was Trustee.

Book 52, page 567, makes final the sale by Jubilee Auction of George Cumby's farm to Marie Coleman.

Book 53, page 337, records how James and Emily Cumbae [that spelling] defaulted on the above agreement, resulting in the property being sold for $315.70 to William Puryear. That tidbit will help as I try to trace the deed.

There were several more references that I will try to summarize later, the most interesting of which describes Thomas Cumby as a resident of Halifax County and Martha as a resident of Mecklenburg in 1851.Thomas and Martha were separated by then, or Thomas, already an old man, was working, perhaps as an overseer, in Halifax County.

Sam"

From **Mecklenburg County Deed Book 33**, p. 521:

Cumby to Cumby Deed, I Thomas Cumba of the County of Halifax and State of Virginia do relinquish to my wife Martha C Cumba of the County of Mecklenburg and State of Virginia, the entire legacy that may be coming to her from her father's estate, or any legacy that she may be entitled to from any person. I also relinquish to her all the property now in her possession, except the interest I may have in the land she now lives on, which interest I except. As witness my hand and seal this 25th day of February 1851. Thomas Cumba   X   his mark.

Another deed began to be recorded on the same page, 521, and maybe it gives a clue toward the answer to your question.

This Deed made this 29th April 1851 between Thomas Cumby and Patsy his wife, And James W. Edmondson. Witnesseth that for and in consideration of the sum of one hundred and ten Dollars, in hand paid by the said James Edmondson, we have bargained and sold, by these presents do bargain and sell unto the said James W. Edmondson all our rights title and interest in the estate of Zachariah Curtis dec'd. Being a legacy of one hundred and fifty Dollars, which be coming to the said Patsy C. Cumby, after the death of her mother Sarah F Curtis, the widow of the said Zachariah Curtis- To have and to

P. 522- hold the said interest to the said James W. Edmondson against the claim- our selves and our heirs, and of all other persons whatsoever-witness our signatures and seals this day above written. Martha C. Cumby

The **biographies of the children of Robert and Mary Cumbia** are derived primarily from the recollections of my mother, Louise Whitby, and her sister, Evelyn Black, as well as my own memories. The dates are in the family Bible.

An email from Cousin Willie Munn-

"Hello Sam, hope you and the family are all well.
I ran across something today I thought was interesting. Went to the Granville NC home page at rootsweb.com and found some interesting reading material about the early residents. You probably have been there before but it was new to me.

Do we know the name of the Tucker that Martha Curtis was married to
before she married Wm Thomas Cumby? In a list of marriages on the Granville site I found a Martha C. Curtis marriage to Robert C. Tucker
on 09 Nov 1824.

We know that Martha C. Tucker (widow) married Wm Thomas Cumby on 07 Oct
1839 which would have been about 15 years later than the first marriage.

I didn't have this information on her first husband's name before now and thought maybe it was new to you also.

later,
willie

MARTHA CURTIS TUCKER:
Library Of Virginia **Bonds and Consents**:
"This is to certify that I have consented to marry Wm Thomas Cumby....., given under my
hand this 7th day of October 1839". Martha C. Tucker (widow).

Martha Curtis was a widow of unknown Tucker at time of marriage to
Thomas Cumby."

1850 Census of Mecklenburg County, 98th District-
Family 546-
James Pritchard 30,
Catharine Pritchard 25
James   "   7,
Elizabeth   "   4,
Heartwell Johnson 48,
Heartwell Arnold - Methodist minister
572-
Mary Wells   65,

Mary Wells	30,
Edward Wells	25,
Harriett Wells	20,
579-	
Alexander Crow	46,
Eliza "	35,
Wm. "	17,
Emily "	14,
Lethe "	12,
Robert "	8,
Virginia "	5,
Angelina Crow	10/12
620-	
Thos. Cumby	75,
Martha C. "	41,
Green "	9,
Louisa "	6,
Lucy Ann "	3,
Alex. Tucker	17,
Selina C. "	16,
Martha P. "	14,
623-	
George Cumby-	45,
Pamelia "	36,
Ann Eliza "	16,
James "	14,
Mary "	12,
John "	10,
Wm "	7.

I looked for 1860 Census data for Mecklenburg County.
James Cumby lived in the County, near the Wells family, but
I could find no record of George A.Cumby and family living
in Mecklenburg in 1860. Dorothy Cumbea's notes mention
George, Pamelia, Louisa, and Robert Cumby living in the

same household, presumably in Mecklenburg. I have not been able to find Dorothy's source or to confirm her findings in regard to the George Cumby family in 1860.

In 1860, according to Dinwiddie County Census, Martha C. Cumby lived in Dinwiddie. She was 49 years old, a seamstress, with a personal estate of $25. With her were Lucy Ann, 12, and Virginia, 10. I checked the Bureau of Vital Statistics for Dinwiddie County, 1853-1860, for the death of Thomas Cumby, but I did not find it.

1860 Census of Mecklenburg County, microfilm at LVA-

James Cumby was 22, lived with Mary Wells, 70, and Mary Wells, 32, and Harriet W., 25. I searched this Census twice to look for George A. Cumby and family, but I could not find them. Family 568 had a "Gnee" Cumby [Green?], 18, farm laborer, in the home of Wm. Roffel.

1870 Census of Mecklenburg County, microfilm at LVA-
Buckhorn Township-
FN - Name, Age-

FN	Name		Age
133-Wells,	Mary T.,		51
" - " ,	Harriett E.,		40
" -Brooks,	Mary S.,		30
" - " ,	David H.,		2
" - " ,	Mary E.,		1
111-Cabiness,	Paschal Y.,		31
" "	, Ann E.	,	35
" "	, James H.	,	10
" "	, John L.	,	8
" "	, William	,	6
" "	, Robert C.	,	4
" "	, Gelbertha,		1

```
"                  , Claiborne , Sally   18
122- Cumby , James,                 33
"          "      , Emily F.,          32
"          "        George A.,         1,
113- Cumby, George   ,              58,
"     -    "    , Pamelia ,           51,
"     -    "    , Louisa   ,          17,
"     -    "    , Robert   ,          12,
241 -      "    , Martha C.,          60,
"       Morgan, Edward,               6,
242        "    , George T. ,         30,
"     -    "    , Lucy J.   ,         21. [ Lucy J. should
```

probably read Lucy A., for elsewhere it has been established that George Morgan married Lucy Ann Cumby.]

I first encountered the 1850 and 1870 Censuses and the 1870 map at http://www.rootsweb.com/~vamecklen/index.htm. That is the address of VaGenWeb's Mecklenburg County Virginia Genealogy Project. I verified the Census data and saw an original map at the Library of Virginia. Carolyn Davis gave me a copy.

The Mormon genealogy page address is http://www.familysearch.org/ .

1880 Census of Mecklenburg County-
Family and Dwelling 203-

```
Alexander Griffin, WM,      42, Farmer, VA,
Sallie F.        "     WF,   44, Wife,
Mary A.        "     WF,   21, Daughter,
Margaret A. "     WF,   18, Daughter,
Sallie W.     "     WF,   13    ",
Johnnie      "     WM,   11, Son,
Thomas E.   "     WM,   9, Son,
Nancy A.     "     WF,   7, Dtr,
Joseph A.    "     WM,   3, Son .
```

Mary A. married Robert Allen Cumbia. Her surname was spelled in various ways, and later it was usually Griffith.

Family no. 349 (South Hill Magisterial District)-Cabbiness, Waddy, WM, 41, keeping house. This may have been the Waddy "Cavendish" who was a hermit and lived for awhile in a small cave near Brodnax, VA.

Buckhorn District, family 249- Cumba, Martha C., 74, Keeping house; Morgan, Edward C., 15, farm laborer; Simmons, Emma, 18, at home. Martha was the widow of Thomas Cumby, and George was her grandson by her daughter Lucy Ann and Lucy's husband George Morgan.

Mecklenburg County Marriage Licenses, LVA Pos. Reel 81, 1870-72-
Found the marriage of George A. Cumby, 60, and Lucy M. Tucker, 28. Husband's parents were "Thomas Cumbey and Agnes his wife", occupation of husband was farmer. Lucy's parents were Merrit and Martha Tucker. George and Lucy married on Dec.19, 1872, at the residence of Miss Mary Tucker and were married by Wm. Carter, Minister M.E.C. Both parties were identified as being widowed. George's place of birth was Campbell County, Lucy's was Mecklenburg.

General Index to Deeds, Mecklenburg County, Virginia, 1765-1933-
January 1838 – George Combey (Grantee), Wm.H. Hurt (Grantor), **Bk 27**, p. 402;
August 15, 1887- J.L.Cumbea (Grantee), Mary T. Wells (Grantor)- **Bk 47**, p 232;
November 21, 1892 – J.L.Cumbea (Grantee), Harriet Wells (Grantor) – **Bk 51**, p.564; [" On Nov. 14, 1892 James

L.Cumbea bought for $250 interest of any kind from Harriet
E. Wells in the tract of land adjoining the lands of J H Gooch
& others"]
March 14, 1911 – R.A. Cumbia (Grantee), R.R.
Jones,Jr.(Grantor) **Bk 74**, p. 163.

**From [Deed] Book 47 p. 232 J.L. Cumbea-Mary T. Wells
et al-**
" Whereas Mary T. Wells and Harriet E. Wells of
Mecklenburg County are growing old and infirm and are
desirous of securing for themselves all proper care and
support and to have an assurance of all services and
attentions necessary to be rendered to and for them during
their lives and the life of the survivor of them; and whereas
their nephew , J. L. Cumbea, is willing to render them such
services and to take such care of them, and to make all proper
and necessary provisions for them, during their lives and the
life of the survivor of them in consideration that they will
convey to him the tract of land now owned and occupied by
them lying in Mecklenburg County Va adjoining the lands of
J.T. Crenshaw[,]Julia A Ray and others containing some 154
acres. Now therefore this deed made this 13th July 1887
between the said Mary T. and Harriet E. Wells of the first
part and J.L. Cumbea of the second part: Witnesseth that for
and in consideration of the promises the parties of the first
part do hereby grant and convey unto said Cumbea the
aforesaid tract of land; subject however to the conditions and
limitations herein specified. The said grantors are to have and
hold the possession and use of the dwelling yard and other
houses now used and occupied by them, and such patch or
patches of ground for garden and other such purposes as they
may desire; also necessary pasturage for 2 head cattle and 2
hogs.
Said Cumbea agrees and obligates himself, to care for and
support his said aunts and the survivor of them during their

lives; that he is annually to furnish them with 2 barrells of flour 3 barrells corn 2 shoats for fattening; to provide them with wood; to do what hauling plowing and going to mill they may desire and to take proper care to render proper services, and, to procure all necessary medical attention to and for them and the survivor of them during their lives and the life of the survivor; and if necessary to supply them with meat; he shall also pay taxes on the land and have each of the said aunts decently buried. And it is distinctly agreed that the said tract of land is specially charged with the payment of the costs and charges of the goods and articles to be furnished and the things to be done hereunder by said Cumbea. And it is also agreed and understood, that if said Cumbea shall at anytime fail to comply with any or either of the terms and stipulations hereof then this conveyance shall at the option of the grantor or either of them be null and void; and in addition thereto, the said Cumbea shall forfeit to the grantors or the survivor of them the sum of $ 50 annually which sum he agrees to pay in the event he shall neglect and refuse to comply with the terms & conditions of this deed, and as to any liability he may incur by reason of the violation of the terms of this deed, he waives the benefit of the homestead exemption. Witnesseth the following signatures & seals this 13 July 1887.

Witness

Chas. T. Reekes   Mary T. Wells   X her mark
J.S. Coleman   Harriet E. Wells
                         J.L. Cumbea

Mecklenburg County Chancery Court records that mention Cumby family-
Sallie J. Cumby vs. E. G. Cumby, 1873-006 cc;
Edward L. Wells Etc. vs. Mary T. Wells Etc.,   1874-060 cc;
Pattie Nanny vs. Adm. of Tucker Etc., 1875-030 cc;
Adm. of Jones vs. Griffin Nanny, 1875-030 cc;

Adm. of Jones vs. Adm. of Tucker Etc., 1875-030 cc;
Exrs. Of E. A. Drumright vs. George Cumby Etc., 1875-079 cc;
Hutcheson Etc. vs. Richardson, 1879-021 cc.

An email sent to interested family members:

"The following is a document that I found in the lawsuit of **Drumwright vs. George Cumby**: [punctuation (or lack of it!), as I found it]

'This deed made the 1st day of November 1860 between George Cumby & his wife Pamela [that spelling] Cumby of the one part Robert A. Walker of the other part wherewith that the said George Cumby and wife doth grant unto the said Robt A Walker the following property towit The tract of land on which said George Cumby now resides containing one hundred acres more or less located on Saffolds Road in the county of Mecklenburg it being the lands bought of Thos. Keeton. One sorrel horse, 4 cows and calves 5 head of hogs 5 head of sheap The entire crop of every description grown or made the present year all the household & kitchen furniture tools of every description. In trust to secure the payment of the following debts, to wit, an execution in favor of Thos. Keeton's Estate for the sum of two hundred & forty one dollars and ninety five cents with interest thereon from the 30th of Novr 1860 til paid off by Charles S. Hutcherson also the sum of fifty dollars due said C.S. Hutcherson by bond and the further sum of about eighty dollars due the Estate of James W. Edmonson & said C.S. Hutcherson assumed the payment of , to save the costs of suit, It shall be lawful that the said Ro A, Walker Trustee shall at any time by giving thirty days notice at public auction proceed to sell the for cash the above named property or a sufficiency thereof to pay said debts and costs, witness the following signatures & seals this first day of November 1860

Teste   George Cumby X his
mark

                                   Pamela Cumby   '

There is more, including Pamela's being 'examined
privily& and apart from her husband' and the finding
that she 'did wish to retract it' [I don't know all the
ramifications of this]. I will try to scan the document and
send it to interested parties.

Eventually, in 1875, the farm was sold to partially satisfy
the debt, which was more than all George's property was
worth.

I spent about two hours closely reading the suit of which
the above is part, also reading a suit brought against Col.
Hutcherson, in which George Cumby gave a very
interesting deposition. A less than flattering picture of
Hutcherson is beginning to emerge more clearly. If my
reading is correct, George had good reason to believe that
he had earned enough money to pay his debts. Col.
Hutcherson did not pay him all that he owed him, and
George believed that the money he was not paid was
money that was going toward his debts. It also is fairly
clear that Hutcherson knew that Confederate money was
worthless or nearly so, for he allegedly refused to accept
it in payment for the debt that George Cumby owed him,
when George, according to his testimony, specifically
tried to pay him off. George Cumby worked as an
overseer during the War Between the States, and he was
paid in Confederate money. I don't have time to type up
the notes now, but later I will try to do so, and you can
have a better idea of what George earned and how much
he actually was paid.

Something else that is evident is just how easy it was for
someone with money and some education to take

advantage of someone with neither. I'm no lawyer, and my head hurt after reading these cases."

The following is part of an email sent to interested family members:

"The following is **George Cumby's' deposition**, given in the case of Richardson vs. Hutcheson, 1879, Mecklenburg County Chancery [now the Circuit] Court:

'Geo. Cumby called by Deft. being sworn deposes and says. -
Question by Defts. counsel- State any conversation which you may have heard between Chas. S. Hutcheson , on of the Plffs. in this suit, and the Deft. Richardson in regard to the receiving by Hutcheson of Confederate currency in payment of certain bonds, which it is claimed by Richardson were assigned by him to Hutcheson in payment for the land in the proceedings mentioned , and as near as you can the time of such conversation?

Answer- Myself and Richardson were out here in the courtyard in conversation and Col. Hutcheson stepped up to Richardson and touched him and says he I can't receive the money. Richardson's reply was to him that you must receive that money in payment for the land. and then Hutcheson's reply was to him again that he couldn't receive it - it was of no service to him - that the children were over in the yankee lines and he couldn't get the money to them. Well, says Richardson to him you must receive this money or secure those bonds for the land I'm living on to make me safe [.] I left them and that was as well as I recollect either in the latter part of the summer or the first of the fall of 1863. - The reason I remember so well is that I had a short time before applied to Col. Hutcheson for a settlement and he refused to receive Confederate money from me and my attention was directed to them to see how they would make it.'

There is another question and answer which I will try to email later, in a day or two.

The above throws a little more light on the economic problems of George's family during the Civil War. Imagine working all season and being paid in money that was no good, then imagine trying to pay your debts with it, and you may appreciate the predicament."

Timeline provided by Willie Munn-

On 1842 Jan 2, E G Cumby was born.

1850-Margaret Effie "Dinks" Crowder was born in Mecklenburg County, Virginia.

1868 Feb 26   E G Cumby and Sally J Tucker marry.

1868   E G deserts wife Sally first time as stated by James E Winkler deposition (9/30/1873)

1868   E G and Dinks leave the neighborhood for 3 years as stated by J E Winkler deposition 9/30/1873.

1869   Attorneys court petition (10/4/1873) says E G deserted Sally in 1869, lived with Dinks and later reconciled with Sally.

1872 Feb   E G & Sally last separation. John R Williams in deposition (9/30/1873) states they last separated 1872 Feb.

1872 Nov 5   Martha Roberta "Pattie Lee" Cumby born at Salem Virginia.

1873 June 24   E G summoned to appear in court the first Monday in July to answer divorce bill exhibited against him.

1873 Jul 7 E G acknowledges summons for divorce case.

1873 Sept 19   James Winkler, Geo Morgan, John Williams, and Geo Cumby summoned for depositions on Sept 30.

1873 Sept 30   Depositions given by Geo Cumby, John R. Williams and James E. Winkler.

1873 Oct 4 Attorneys Lee & Thorp petition the court for annulment of E G and Sally marriage.

1873 Oct 23   Depositions given by Samel Fai.ar and G T Morgan. Both state currently lives in house at night.

1873 Oct 24   Divorce granted to E G Cumby and Sally Tucker.

1874 Feb 9   Tom Cumby born, son of E G and Dinks so tombstone says.

1880 Dec 14   E G Cumba and Margarette Crowder marry in Warren Co. NC, age 27 (b. 1853?), parents Thomas T and Mary.

1919 Apr 27   E G Cumby died.

1932 May 3   Tom Cumby died, son of E G and Dinks. Death cert. maiden name of mother Clayborne.

The following documents are of the divorce proceedings of Edward Green Cumby and his first wife Sally J. Tucker.
Transcriber, Willie G. Munn-Permission given orally by Willie Munn on 7/20/11-

Divorce Proceedings of Cumby vs. Cumby, as transcribed by Willie Munn:

I hereby acknowledge legal service of the within
Summons July 7th 1873

his
E G X Cumby
mark

Witness   Wm. A. Carter Shiff [Sheriff]

cir co [circuit court] *See & Thorp*   *264*

Cumby

vs } Spa in Chancery

Cumby

*   10*
July Rules 1873
To E G Cumby

Take notice that on Thursday September 30th 1873 between
the hours of 6 am to 6 pm of that day I shall at the law
office of W T Atkins in Boydton proceed to take the
deposition
of Jas Winckler & this to be read as evidence in a suit

in the Circuit Court of Mecklenburg in which I am plff
[plaintiff]
and you are defe [defendant]. *And if the said deposition be
not completed in that day they will be continued from
day to day until completed.*

> *Sally J Cumby,*
> *By Counsel.*

COMMONWEALTH OF VIRGINIA –
>   To the Sheriff of Mecklenburg

County Greeting:
WE [faded and unreadable] YOU TO SUMMON *James Winkler.
Jepee[?] Morgan. Geo
Morgan. John Williams & Geo A Cumby*

>   *Commissioner W T Atkins at his office in Boydton*

on the
personally to appear before ~~the judge of the~~   ~~Court~~
~~of~~ Mecklenburg County,
~~at the Court House thereof, on the~~ *30*[th] day of *September
1873* ~~Term next~~, to testify
and the truth to say in behalf of *Sally J Cumby*

in a certain matter of controversy in our said court, before our
said Judge, depending and on and undermined between
Said Sally J Cumby Plff [plaintiff] *and E. G. Cumby deft*
[defendant]

and this *they* shall in nowise omit under the penalty of £100.

And have then and there this writ. Witness,
RUTLEDGE P. HUGHES, Clerk of Court of our said court at office,
This *19th* day of *September* , 1873 , and in the 98*th* year of the Commonwealth.

Teste:

A P Hughes Clerk.

THE COMMONWEALTH OF VIRGINIA –
To the Sheriff of Mecklenburg County, Greetings:
WE COMMAND YOU TO SUMMON *E G Cumby*

to appear on the first Monday in *July* next, (being rule day,) at the Clerk's Office
of the *Circuit* Court for the County of Mecklenburg, to answer a bill exhibited against
him in the said Court by *Sallie J Cumby (who was before her Marriage Sallie J Tucker)*

And unless *he* shall answer the said bill within one month thereafter, the Court will
take the same for confessed and decree accordingly; and this
he shall in no wise omit
under the penalty of £100.

And have then and there this writ. Witness, Rutledge Ph. Hughes, Clerk of our said Court, at office this *24th* day of *June* , 1873 , and in the 97*th* year of the Commonwealth.

Teste, *A P*

Hughes Clerk

21 Cir Co [Circuit Court] *See & Thorp*

Cumby Sallie J   *Cumby*

vs   *}Bill & exhibits*   *vs*
} Bill --

E. G. Cumby
      Cumby

1873. July Rules Bill & exhibits
filed Spa via Returned Service
acknowledged by deft [defendant]
1873 August Rules Set for hearing
on the bill taken for Confessid [?]
1873 Oct <u>Term Final</u>
The depositions of Geo. A. Cumby and others taken before
me, W Baskerville, a Notary Public for the county of
Mecklenburg and State of Virginia taken at the office of
Counselor Atkins in the town of Boydton, pursuant to notice,
to be read as testimony in behalf of the Plff [Plaintiff] *in a*
certain suit in equity depending in the Circuit Court of
Mecklenburg in which Sally Cumbie is Plff and E G. Cumby
Deft [Defendant] *taken this the 30 day of September 1873.*

      Present A. S. See   Counsel for Plff &
          E.G. Cumby   Deft

Deponent Geo. A. Cumby being sworn deposes and says
Question by Plff. counsel -- State anything you may know in
regard to the Plff and Deft in this suit, having formerly lived
and cohabitated together as man and wife in the County of
Mecklenburg Virginia, of the Deft E. G. Cumby having
deserted the Plff his wife and living separate and apart from

her. State also the circumstances under which this separation occurred and how long it has continued?

Answer – The Plff and Deft lived together as man and wife. I lived in the same neighborhood with them. I don't know the cause of the separation, but they have separated. It has been about four years ago since their separation I think. They separated several times, but the last separation was on account of the Deft taking up with one Dink Crowder, as was stated by the Plff, but whether he took up with Dinks Crowder or not, I am not able to say.

Question by same – State whether or not you have not heard the Plff in this suit, declare or state in the presence of the Deft E. G. Cumby, that the reason of her desiring to obtain a divorce from him, was the conduct of E. G. Cumby her husband, in having repeatedly deserted and neglected her, and living in adultery with the woman called Dinks Crowder, and if the Deft made any denial of the charge of adultery thus made against him by the Plff?

Answer – A few days before the Plff commenced this suit and in the day she was in Mr. Sees office for that purpose, the Plff said then and there in the presence of the Deft E. G. Cumby, that the reason she wanted to be divorced from the Deft, was that he had been living in adultery with Dinks Crowder and they had gone off together and remained away three years, and when the Deft and said Dinks Crowder came back, they brought two children which she believed to be the result of said adultery. and I don't think he made any denial of it in Mr. Sees office.

Question by same – State if you have not heard the Deft, E. G. Cumby admit that he had been guilty of adultery since his marriage to the Plff.

Answer – We were talking about it and he said to me, that she could not prove that he had committed adultery, and he *said he would admit before the court that he had committed adultery provided it would not subject him to a prisontment [imprisonment], but he would say that he committed adultery, but did not say who with.*

Question by same – In your answer to a previous question you have stated that you resided in the same neighborhood with the Plff and Deft, at the time of the desertion of the former by the latter; now state whether or not, the Deft E. G. Cumby, and the woman Dinks Crowder did not both absent themselves from the County of Mecklenburg at or about the same time, and did not both return to to it either together or about the same time, after a long period of absence from said county.

Answer – They left the neighborhood about the same time, whether together or not I don't know. And they returned to the county and neighborhood again about the same time but I can't say whether they came back together or not. Both were absent some two or three years.

Question by same – State whether or not the Plff in this suit is not in poor and necessitous circumstances; if her said husband; the Deft in this suit, had not failed to make any mohes [?] provision for her, and if she has not been compelled for several years, owing which the desertion of her said husband has lasted, to rely upon her own labor and exertions to gain the means of a livelihood?

Answer – She is a poor woman, and has had no means of support, owing the period named, except by her own labor.
                    and further deponent saith not.

                         his
                    Geo. X A. Cumby
                         mark

<u>2</u>

Deponent John R Williams being duly sworn deposes and says

Question by Plff counsel – State anything you may know in reference to the Plff and the Deft in this suit, having lived and cohabbitted together as man and wife in the County of Mecklenburg, at a time subsequent to the year 1868. State also anything you may know in regard to the Defts having deserted the Plff in company with the woman Dinks Crowder. About how long did this desertion last, and all you may know about it?

Answer – I know the Plff and Deft lived together as man and wife, subsequent to the year 1868. I know that the Deft and the said Dinks Crowder were missing from the neighborhood, but whether they went together I don't know. I know also that they were both back in the neighborhood, but do not know whether they returned together. They were absent about three years, I think. They were both missing at or about the same time. After this return the Plff and Deft went to living together and housekeeping, and after a little while they again separated.

Question by same – State whether since the last separation, mentioned by you, the Plff and Deft, have at any time lived together as husband and wife?

Answer – They have not lived together since as man and wife, which last separation occurred about the month of February 1872. [Martha Roberta "Pattie Lee" Cumby was born 5 November 1872, nine months later in Salem Virginia so states the Munn family Bible.]

Question by same – Do you know the cause assigned for this last and final separation between the Plff and the Deft?
Answer – No I do not know the cause of it, more than I heard the Deft say he could not live with the Plff in peace.

And further this deponent saith

not.

his
*John R. **X** Williams*
mark

Deponent James E Winkler being duly sworn deposes and says

Question by Plff counsel – State anything you may know of the Deft having deserted his wife the Plff in this suit, about what time and under what circumstances this desertion occurred – State also anything you may know of the Deft having taken up and lived in adultery with the woman Dinks Crowder, or any other woman, and state everything you know in regard to the last and final separation between the Plff and Deft?

Answer – They were living at my plantation at my house, on my plantation at the time of the first separation. the Plff sent for me to know what to do, and said, the Deft had said he was going off and take Dinks Crowder with him, never to return, and wished me to advise her what to do. I advised her to go back to her father, which she did, in the year 1868, I think. I know nothing of his, the Deft, taking up with Dinks Crowder, but they left the neighborhood about the same time and returned about the same time, after an absence of about three years. About the last and final separation, I know nothing of its cause.

Question by same – State any admission or statement you may have heard the Deft E. G. Cumby make in regard to his having committed adultery?

Answer – He said to me he had been accused of it, but that no one knew of it. At the time he said this he was living with the Plff his wife.

Question by the same – Do you now live in the same neighborhood with the Plff. and do you not know that she is in poor and necessitous circumstances, and that since the last desertion of her by the Deft her husband, she has been dependant on her own labor and exertions to obtain the means of her lively hood?
Answer – I do live in the same neighborhood with the Plff. She is in poor and needy circumstances and dependent upon her labor and exertions to obtain a lively hood.
And further the deponent saith not.

James E Winkler

The foregoing depositions were sworn to and subscribed to before me this the 30th November 1873.
Wm Baskerville Jr
Notary Public

The taking of the foregoing depositions is postponed to Friday the 3rd day of October 1873, at which time the taking will be resumed at this office.
W. Baskerville Jr
N.P.
Oct 3rd 1873

No other witness appearing the taking of these depositions is concluded
Wm T. Atkins
NP

Cumby Sally J

vs   } Depositions

E. G. Cumby

*1873 Sept 30th Returned by
Court & filed*

[The following two depositions are faded and difficult to read.]

The deposition of Samuel G Farmer [?] and others taken before ... W Baskerville Jr a Notary Public for the county of Mecklenburg at my office in Boydton on the 24 th day of October 1873, by consent of parties by counsel to be read as evidence in behalf of the Plff in a suit in Chancery depending in the Circuit Court of Mecklenburg of Cumby vs Cumby – Present Thorp for Plff & Baskerville for Deft

Deponent Samel [?] G Farmer [?] being duly sworn deposes and says.

Question by Plff Counsel –
State how far do you live from the house occupied by Dinks Crowder and whether it is a matter of general notoriety in the neighborhood that the Deft E. G. Cumby constantly lives in adultery with the said Dinks Crowder and sleeps with her generally in her house?
Answer – I live in about ¾ of a mile of the house now occupied by Dinks Crowder and it is a matter of general notoriety in the neighborhood that the said E. G. Cumby lives in adultery with her and generally stays at her house at night. I know of no other person living in the house with the said Dinks Crowder except her children.
                    And further deponent sayith not.

                    S .. Fai.ar

G.T. Morgan being sworn deposes and says.

Question by Plff Counsel –

Do you live in the neighborhood of the house now occupied by Dinks Crowder and is it not a matter of general notoriety and universally believed in the neighborhood that the Def Cumby is now constantly living in adultery with the said Dinks Crowder, staying in her house at night and having his washing done by her?

Answer –

I live in about a mile and a half of said house, and it is a matter of general notoriety and belief that the said E. G. Cumby now lives with the said Dinks Crowder in a state of adultery and stays at her house and has his washing done at her house.

And further deponent saith not

his
G. T. X Morgan
mark

The following depositions were transcribed and sworn to before me the date and year above written.

W. Baskerville Jr
N.P.

To the Hon A. D. Dickinson Judge of the Circuit Court of Mecklenburg. In Chancery differing.

Humbly complaining shewith unto your Honor your Complainant Sallie J. Tucker, (who before her marriage hereinafter mentioned) was Sallie J. Tucker, in the year 1868. intermarried with E.G. Cumby, Defendant, in this County where both your Complainant and the said E. G. Cumby resided : that in the year 1869. the said E. G. Cumby deserted your Complainant and lived in a State of Adultery with a certain lewd prostitute Dinks Crowder, by name : that afterwards your Complainant became reconciled to her said husband E.G. Cumby, professing faith in his promises of amendment and that he would forever cease to have intercourse with the said prostitute.

But now so if it may it please your honor, her said husband E.G. Cumby, has again desterted [deserted] your Complainant to live in open and lewd Adultery with the said Prostitute called Dinks Crowder, with whom your Complainant charges that he does now live in a State of Adultery. Altogether failing and refusing in any way to provide for the most necessary wants of your Complainant.

Your Complainant shewith further unto your Honor, that since this last mentioned act of desertion and adulterous intercourse, she has never become reconciled to her said husband nor has she since this last mentioned time and acts of adultery lived or cohabitated with him.

Shewith further unto your Honor that your Complainant is poor and in needy circumstances. That by reason of her being the wife of the said E.G. Cumby is unable to support herself by offering decent employment which she could easily do if separated from him.

Your Complainant therefore urges your Honor that her said marriage may be annulled.

And that your Honor will grant her a decree of divorce from the bond of matrimony with her said husband; that E. G. Cumby be made a party defendant to this Bill and ordered to answer on oath its allegations. And that your Honor will grant all such other further and more general relief in the provides as to your Honor may deem just and the particular Equity of the Case may require.
Aud te [unreadable]

Lee & Thorp

[in a different hand]
Sworn to by Sally J Cumby before me this the 4th day of Oct 1893

A P Hughes clk

[clerk]

Sally J. Cumby   Plff [Plaintiff]

vs   *Decree*

E.G. Cumby   *Deft* [Defendant]

    This cause which had been regularly matured at Rules and Sch [scheduled] *for hearing on this day to be heard upon the Bill, exhibits, and the examination of wit nesser, and was argued by counsel; on consideration whereof the court being of opinion that the charge of adultery and desertion against the defendant is fully proved independently of the admissions of the deft* [defendant] *doth adjudge order and decree that the marriage heretofore solemnized between E. G. Cumby and Sally J. Cumby be and the same divorced from his wife the said Sally J. Cumby and all the right title and interest of the said Sally J. Cumby in and to the estate real and personal not of the said E.G. Cumby shall henceforth cease and determine; and that the plaintiff recover from the defendant her costs by her expended in the prosecution of this suit and nothing further remaining to be done in this suit, it is or decred* [decreed] *that the same be removed from the docket but leave in reserved to the parties to make application to the court for such further orders as are authorized by same.*

Notes by Sam Whitby on divorce of Sallie and Green-

Sallie Cumby sued Green Cumby for divorce, alleging adulterous relations between Green and Dinks Crowder, with whom Green had two children. Documentation includes testimony of George Cumby and others. Divorce was granted.

October,1873- E.G. Cumby ..." deserted your complainant and lived in a state of adultery with a certain lewd prostitute , Dinks Crowder by name"..." reconciled...professing faith in his promises"... "to cease to have intercourse with the said prostitute." "E.G. Cumby has again deserted your complainant to live in open and lewd adultery."

George Cumby's deposition alleged that Green had stayed out of state 2 o3 years with Dinks Crowder and returned with 2 children. Lucy Cumby Morgan's, husband, George, was a witness for the complainant.

George Cumby's deposition includes the following: "The Plff and Deft lived together as man and wife. I lived in the same neighborhood with them. I don't know the cause of their separation, but they have separated. It has been about four years ago since their separation I think. They separated several times, but the last separation was on account of the Deft taking up with one Dinks Crowder, as was stated by the Plff, but whether he took up with Dinks Crowder or not, I am not able to say."

James Winkler, John Williams, J. Morgan, George Morgan, and Geo. A. Cumby gave depositions. James Winkler said. " They were living at my plantation at my house...at the time of their first separation 1868 I think...[and] returned after 3 years."

1875-079 refers to a lawsuit that eventually resulted in the sale of the farm of George Cumby. There are about fifty pages of documentation, including the sworn testimony of George Cumby. Revealed that George Cumby was employed as an overseer for Mrs.Love and that payment was not made on a series of loans secured by the family farm. One of the documents contains what may be Mrs. George Cumby's signature, which looks like "Pamela." The farm was ordered sold at Jubilee Auction, and it . was sold in November, 1874, when it was bought by Marie H. Coleman for $ 311.50 in cash, the highest bidder.

1874-060 CC- Edward L. Wells Etc.vs Mary T. Wells Etc. – " Your complainants Edward L. Wells, George H. Wells, Jas. L. Cumby, Jn. Cumby, P.Y Cabaness and Ann his wife, David G. Brooks and Mary his wife, Louisa Cumby and Robert Cumby an infant under the age of 21 who sues by Geo Cumby his father and next friend...." Two parcels of land in Mecklenburg County, 117 acres and 53 acres, were to be sold according to the Will of Henry Wells at the elder Mary Wells' death. The property was sold. $48.56 was left over after expenses, and the money was divided among the complainants. [This entry indicates that Pamelia Wells Cumby and Mary Wells were deceased by the time of the legal action.] This morning I looked at some deeds at the Library of Virginia, in which Cumby ancestors were listed as Grantors.

An email sent 7/28/04-
"In Deed Book 29, on page 538, I found an agreement in 1842 by Thomas Cumbie [one of the very few times I have found that spelling] with Drury H. Lett et al [Chesley Curtis], a Deed of Trust putting up as collateral **Thomas's farm and property in Lunenburg County**. The agreement is clearly written but fairly lengthy. It can be summarized by

saying that Thomas owed numerous merchants who wanted to be paid. Thomas's property was described as follows: "1 sorrel mare & colt 1 cow. 3 ploughs. 2 coulter ploughs, 4 hill hoes, 4 grub hoes, 1 Loom [illegible] sitting chairs 2 spinning wheels 7 beds & furniture 2 bed steads 2 tables 1 Doz Table Knives & forks 2 dishes 2 pitchers, 1 doz: plates, 2 ovens 2 pots 1 Coffee pot 1 spider [?] 1 set cups and saucers[and] a certain tract or parcel of land lying and being in the County of Lunenburg [200 acres, 150 acres life estate and 50 acres fee simple, whatever that means]." The deal basically was that Thomas would pay up or his property would be sold. I have not seen for sure how this turned out, but I can guess.

Book 41, page 575, records the sale in 1877 by E.G.[Green] Cumby of his interest in Martha C. Curtis's 100 acres, for $25 to W.C.Curtis and James Edmonson. It describes Martha's property as "bounded in the North by Estate of Z. Curtis & W.C. Curtis, on the East by Giles Bowens' Est., on the South by Stony Cross road, and on the west by J.W.Edmonson's Est."

Book 51, page 565 records a Deed of Trust by which James and Emily Cumbea bought 154 acres from Harriett Early Wells for $250. Warner Wells was Trustee.

Book 52, page 567, makes final the sale by Jubilee Auction of George Cumby's farm to Marie Coleman.

Book 53, page 337, records how James and Emily Cumbae[that spelling] defaulted on the above agreement, resulting in the property being sold for $315.70 to William Puryear. That tidbit will help as I try to trace the deed.

There were several more references that I will try to summarize later, the most interesting of which describes Thomas Cumby as a resident of Halifax County and Martha as a resident of Mecklenburg in 1851. Either Thomas and Martha were separated by then or Thomas, already an old man, was working, perhaps as an overseer, in Halifax County."

An email sent on 7/28/04:

"Today I followed up on the situation in Mecklenburg Deed Book 29. Lunenburg Book 33, p. 33- 6A, 1842, reveals that Thomas Cumbie owed money to Hutcheson & Reeks, William T. Coleman, Lewis Williams, William Taylor, P. Reekes, Charles O. Harper, Drury H. Lett, Harper & Reeks, and Chesley Curtis. P. 161 deals with the resolution of the aforementioned. Suffice it to say that on June 12, 1843, some property was sold for what looked somewhat like sixty dollars and .25. The deed was very faded, and the handwriting, to me at least, was almost hopeless. Josiah B. Wilson bought the property. Maybe someday I can stop by the courthouse and look at the original, and maybe it will be readable.

I glanced at the **1910 Census of Mecklenburg County**, looking for one thing but finding another. In the LaCrosse Magisterial District, family 235, I found the family of John Robert Cumbea. He was head of household, 44, and his wife, Sallie, was 42. Their children were as follows: Lewis, 15; Nittie, 13 (daughter); Russell, 12; Swanson, 8; Cathellon[sic], 6; Edward, 4; William, 2; and Gilbert, 3/12."

Because his father, Emmit Pulley, was mentioned in Exploring the Cumbia Family Tree, I gave **Charlie Buck Pulley** a copy of it. Charlie Buck **shared some memories of**

his father and my grandfather, Oscar Cumbia, Sr. Charlie Buck said that one of the things he remembered about visiting the Cumbia farm was that it was a quiet and friendly place, without people yelling at each other. He said that he remembered going fishing with the Mr. Pulley and Granddaddy. One place where they liked to fish was Ivory Banks, on Connell land on the Meherrin River. Charlie Buck said that he used to ride in the back of the truck so that he could hop out to open and close gates. He said the older fisherman would tell him he could fish anywhere he wanted to, except for one place, which was always the best fishing spot. Charlie Buck told about Mr. Pulley and Granddaddy fishing at Buggs Island. They used to go out on the rocks behind the dam. Mr. Pulley told Oscar to listen for the horn that would warn them that gates were going to open. When the horn sounded, Mr. Pulley pulled up his gear and started moving to high ground, but Granddaddy said to wait, he was getting a bite. Suddenly he saw his gear floating around him, and he had to make a run for the bank. Another time, they saw a man using a home made, secret bait to catch a lot of fish. Granddaddy asked to examine the bait, and he secretly procured a small sample, which he said he would take home to try to discover its ingredients.

Lunenburg County, Virginia-

From Lunenburg County Marriages- Elizabeth Cumby married William H. Eagles in March, 1815. She was probably a daughter of Thomas and Susanna, possibly a daughter of Thomas and Agnes.

Lunenburg County, deaths-
Nancy Comba died on March 28, 1854. She was 78 years old, born in Campbell County. She died from old age. Info was provided by Wm. Rutledge, her son-in-law.

1880 Census of Lunenburg County, VA-
Columbian Grove, Fam. 58, Household 95-
Cumbie, James, 43, Keeps Mill; Emily, 43, Wife, Keeping house; George 11, Son; Mary, 7, Daughter; Angelina, 5, Daughter; John R., 3, Son; Major H., 2/12, Son, b. in March.

I checked the **Bureau of Vital Statistics for Lunenburg County, 1874-1896**, and I found no Cumbies. The death of Gilbertha Cabiniss was recorded on 15 Dec 1882. She was 14, and she died from chills. Her parents were Phascal and AnaElizza Cabiniss[sic].

From **Lunenburg County VA Deed Book 30, 1833-1837**, p.451-452-
August 26, 1836, Thomas Hutcherson and wife Nancy to Thomas Cumby, all of Lunenburg Co., $ 105, 194; Lunenburg County, Muddy Crk& Meherrin River, adj John Garrott, George Crowder, James Smithson, Jonathon Booker.

An email that I sent to interested family members:

"This afternoon I visited the Library of Virginia and found a few things of interest.

I found an **1871 map of Mecklenburg and Lunenburg Counties**. It identified Muddy Creek. Thomas Cumby owned land at Muddy Creek and the Meherrin River before he married Martha Curtis Tucker and moved to Mecklenburg County. Muddy Creek merges into the Meherrin River downstream from the confluence of the North and South Meherrin Rivers, on the north side of the Meherrin. It is upstream from the Saffolds Road crossing (I am not sure there was a bridge) of the River. This gives us a good idea of where Thomas's farm was. It is probably more than a coincidence that George bought his farm, on Saffolds Road, paying cash in hand, at about the same time that Thomas sold his farm.

There were several mentions of Emmanuel Cumbee in King George County records. He bought 200 acres of land from William McBee in 1730. This Emmanuel could not have been the same person who lived in Campbell in the early 1800s. He may well have been an uncle or some other relative. I have seen the transaction earlier on a Combs family page and elsewhere, with variant spellings. The spelling on the actual document was a clear, incontestable Cumbee, not Combs or Cambee.

I found in **King George Order Books** Margaret Comboy's request to bind out her son, John Byron, in 1727 because she was not able to take care of him. He was bound out to, made the servant of, William Strother until he turned 21. This John may be the same one who turned up later in North Carolina and then Halifax County, VA, and who likely was the father of Thomas Cumbo/Cumby, Sr."

From **Deed Book 31-**
"John Freeman and wife Eliza [paid] toThomas Cumby $50 [for] their ¼ interest in the above property."

From **Lunenburg Guardian Accts 1828-1851-**
Entry dated Nov. 1, 1831 mentions Thos. Cumby " closthers & c rec'd of Thos Cumby rent land, hire Joe/ Clarissa & Henry Reuben" ... "A/C Wm. G Coleman gdn Peter W. Coleman orphan Thos Coleman." From the Lunenburg County Will Book # 9, p. 351, Dec. 6, 1828: mentions estate Peter Epes deed and "Thos Cumby overseer." This mentions that Thomas Cumby was paid from the estate for his services as an overseer.

From **Lunenburg Will Book # 10**, p. 138, Sept. 9, 1831: estate of Sterling Fowlkes, purchasers at estate sale 23 Dec 1828 Thos Combay, carriage tobacco."

From **Lunenburg Will Book # 11**, p. 300, 7 Jul 1838, estate of Robt Bagley decd, "Mrs Cumby flour."

1820 Census of Lunenburg County – no Cumbys were listed on the census.

1830 Census of Lunenburg County (p. 279) - Thomas Cumby, head of household, 1 female 45-50, 3 sons 15-20, 1 son 10-15, 2 children, 1 male and 1 female, 5 or under.

1840 Census of Lunenburg County (p. 6)–Major Cumby was head of household. Lunenburg Deed Book 30, 1833-1837, pp. 120-121, 26 Aug 1834: "Spencer Mulling of Charlotte Co. indebted to Thomas Cumbey & William H. Hurt of Lunenburg Co.... Witnesses...Stephen Davis. PP 451-452, 26 Aug 1836, Thomas Hutcherson & wife Nancy to

Thomas Cumby, all of Lunenburg Co. $ 105, 194 acres; Muddy Creek & Meherrin River, adj John Garriott, George Crowder, James Smithson, Jonathon Booker.

Major Cumby and Nancy Morgan married in Lunenburg County on 13 Oct 1835.[Correction: Oct 13, 1835 was the date the marriage was recorded, by Rev. Daniel Petty, who recorded it "to the best of my(his) recollection."] Sur.Thomas Hutcheson. They were married by Daniel Petty.

1850 Census of Lunenburg County,Family 231-
Asa B. Cabaniss- 50 – farmer
Rebecca S. C.   -49
Esther A. C.   -24
Frances C. C.   -22
James S. C.   -20
Mary R. C.   -17
P. Y. C.   -12- future husband of Ann E. Cumby

W.E. Cabiness, a miller, married Jennie Cabiness on March 14, 1920. He was 55, she was 58 and widowed. W.E.' parents were P.Y. and Ann Eliza Cabiness. Her parents were A.L. and Elizabeth Davis.

C. H. Cabiness, 25, married Clara Irene Mead, 16. He was a son of J.H. and Jennie Cabiness. She was a daughter of V.A. and Minnie D. Mead. For some unknown reason I did not record the date. I didn't even record the county! My memory is that the data came from Lunenburg County.

A book called <u>80% HEAVEN BOUND</u> , deaths and burials in Charles City County, VA mentions several individuals named Cumber, African-American.

Halifax County, Virginia-
From the **Halifax County Deed Book 15**, p. 230-

"I, Thomas Cumbo, have sold and delivered to James Chalmers, 1 bay mare and colt, 3 cows, and 2 2-year-old cattle, 1 sow, and 7 pigs, and 1 1-year-old barrow, all the tobacco on hand, the quantity not ascertained, & all the household furniture that I at this time possess, with the corn in the crib, thought to be thirty barrels, for the sum of 30 pounds four shillings and three pence. Signed Nov 24, 1791 Thomas (his mark X) Cumbo
Wit. John Henry Firesheetz, Emanuel (his mark X) Cumbo
If the said Cumbo pays the 30 pounds, then the within obligation [is] to be void. Signed Nov 24 1791-James Chalmers
Wit. Emanuel Cumbo and John Henry Firesheetz
Recorded Nov 28, 1791 "

The above Thomas Cumbo is possibly Agnes Weatherford's husband, but I think rather that he was the father of Agnes's husband, the Thomas who moved to Campbell County and died in 1817.

I also found a debt of 40 pounds and 19 shillings to James Bruce, secured in 1801 by property belonging to Charles Cumbo: " 124 acres more or less"..." Bounded by land belonging to the following Persons, To Wit, Richard Martin, Pettus Ragland, John Ferguson, & John Perkins's Estate, also 11 head of cattle...." There are numerous other mentions of Charles Cumbo's farm as part of the boundary to other parcels of land. If any of those parcels of land is identified by a map, as likely is the case, one might possibly identify, even today, the parcel of land that belonged to Charles Cumbo. It is impossible so far to say for sure, but my hunch is that

Charles was a brother to Thomas Cumbo/Cumby, Sr., and therefore an uncle to "our" Thomas.

An email sent on Oct. 6, 2004:

"I went to the LVA yesterday to look for the Will of Charles Cumbo of Halifax Co., without success so far. Charles was probably a brother of Thomas Cumbo, Sr., who likely was our Thomas Cumby's father. I did find an inventory of Charles' estate, dated Dec. 10, 1802, and it is as follows: two feather beds and their furniture, ½ dozen earthen plates, 5 small bowls and one quart mug, 2 pewter [illegible] 4 plates and 2 dishes, 4 spoons & 2 small tin cups, 1 chist[sic] and table [very illegible], ½ dozen chairs, 1 [il., perhaps mare] saddle, 1 loom, 1 ole[sic] pot and hook and 1 ole oven, 6 ole hoes 1 cutter [Coulter?] 1 ole cotton wheel, 1 cooking glass, 1 ole pair of cotton & cards, 1 grinden [sic] stone, 1 pitcher and 1 flat [illegible], 1 pole ax, 3 head horses, 2 prs iron traces and collars, 11 head cattle, 15 head hogs, 6 forks and 5 knives, 1 water pail 1 piggin [?] & 1 tub. The inventory was very faded and in an odd handwriting, in other words, very hard to read. In 1824 Elizabeth Cumbo's estate was very similar. She was probably Charles' widow, the former Elizabeth Maschiel. I did notice that she owned a team of oxen. The plan is to keep looking for the Will that supposedly lists Charles and Elizabeth's children.

In the Halifax data at the LVA there are a great many mentions of Charles and Thomas Cumbo. Most of them do not add to our knowledge of the family tree. They consist largely of orders to work on clearing various roads in the County, payment of various taxes, lawsuits, etc. I am still reading the material, and I still hope to find useful sources."

1850 Census of Halifax County, Northern District-
Family 245-
Thomas R. Cumbua –38-boatman,

Eliza	- 37,
Elizabeth	-16,
Phoebe A.	-12,
Harriet	-10,
Margaret A.	- 7,
Louisa	- 5,
Susan	- 3,
Robert	-1,
Horation Rickman	-19, Overseer,
James Wengow	-30, Carpenter,
Turner Scott	-25, Boatman, M,
Masten Chaver	-25, " ",
Richard Jackson	-26, " ,
Joseph Cumbua	-23 ".

246-
Harrison Cumbua, 46, Carpenter,

Sarah A.	25.

220-
Alfred H. Cumba, 37, Boatman,
Family of Alfred Cumba, continued,
Nancy B. Cumba, 37

Permelia	, 15, Student,
Charles B.	, 12,
James M.	,10,
Mary E.	, 8,
John W.	, 6,
Seluda A.	, 1.

588-
Elizabeth Cumba, 39,

Sarah   , 32.

914-
John Cumbo, 48, Farmer,
Ruth   ,   45,
Elizabeth   ,   21,
Ann J.   ,   19,
Lucy   ,   17,
John J.   ,   15,
Edward W. ,   14,
Absolem   ,   13,
Wyley   ,   12,
Nancy   ,   11,
Elisha B.   ,   10,
James W.   ,   7,
Morgan   ,   5.

1850 Census of Halifax County, Southern District-
172-
Polly Cumby, 65,
Harriet   , 40,
Alexander   , 22,
John   , 18,
Mary   , 15

921-
William B. Cumbey, 28,
Elizabeth J.   , 25,
Sarah   , 2,

922-
Letitia Cumbey,   , 50,
Ann   ,   , 30.

Info found on the Mormon Internet page: (let the reader beware) The **1880 Census of Halifax County**, VA, Red Bank, showed the following:

J.J. Cumbie,   47, Head of household, Farmer[a son of John J. and Ruth Cumbo];
Camilla E. C.,   27, Wife, Keeps house [wife of John J. after death of first wife, named Ruth, just like his mother];
George C. C.,   22, Son, [George Calvin];
Martha A. C.,   19, Dtr.;
Elizabeth F. C., 18, Dtr;
Jonus E. C.,   9, Son;
Charles L.,   7, Son;
Ada B. C.,   4, Dtr;
Annie G. C.,   11/12, Dtr.

An email sent to interested family members:

"This morning I looked at the **1910 Census of Halifax County**, VA, and found the following:
Family 109-
George C. Cumbie ,   53, Head;[George Calvin]
Ellen   "   , 29, Wife;
Garnet   "   , 12, Dtr. [seems to be a transposition of the next line, a mistake];
Evelyn   "   , 11, Son [seems to be a mistake];
Herot   "   , 7, Son [perhaps should be Heriot];
Emily   "   , 6, Dtr;
Mary   "   , 4, Dtr:
Briggs   "   , 1, Son.

Family 45-
John Cumbie, 75, Head;
Camilla   " , 63, Wife;
Ethel   " , 18, Dtr.

Family 64-
Arthur Cumbie(illegible), 27, Head;

Virginia (illegible) ",   20, Wife.

Family 105-
Wiley Cumby, 13, Stepson of Lula and Aelis Bliss.

Family 135-
Charlie H. Cumby, 38 , Head;
Seleta A.   "   , 32 , Wife;
Wiley A.   "   , 12 , Son;
Milley   "   , 9, Dtr;
William   "   , 6, Son.

The above will be added to the typed compilation of notes.

Several years ago, when I started researching the family tree and history, I talked to Morris Cumby who lives in Chesterfield County. He is descended from George and Heriot. It's good finally to fill in some gaps and make the linkage."

Some Halifax Co. marriages-

1857, marriage of John J. Cumbie, 24, to Ruth Bradshaw, 17. His parents were John and Ruth Cumbie.

1867, Absolom D. Cumby, son of John and Ruth Cumby, married Martha A. Davis.

1877, Martha R. Cumby, 18, daughter of Alfred and Nancy Cumby, married Joseph Hazelwood.

From _MARRRIAGES OF HALIFAX COUNTY, VIRGINIA: 1801-1831_-
25 January 1830, Prudence H. Cumby married John R. Lester. Sur. Charles Cumby;
25 Dec.1826, Martha Cumbie married Thompson Dunn;

5August 1807, Elizabeth Cumbo to Richard Dyer, signs her own consent;

18 Dec.1816, Charles Cumbie and Nancy Cornwall, md. On Dec.22 by Rev. John Terry;

13 Jan.1818, William Cumbie and Elizabeth Powell. Md.Jan.14 by Rev. David Street;

9 Dec. 1816, Alexander Cumbo and Mary Wilkerson. Md. Same day;

1 June 1806, Peter Cumbo and Dolly Gray, Wit. William Cumbo, Md. Same day;

12 Jan. 1804, Thomas Cumbo & Agnes Wetherford, who signs her own consent.

General Index to Marriages, Halifax County, Males, on microfilm at the LVA-

Thomas Comba md. Agnes Wetherford on Jan. 12, 1804, from Book 1, p. 55;

Charles Combo md. Elizabeth Maschiel on Sept.7, 1786, from
Book 1, p. 9;

Peter Combo md. Dolly Gray on June 1, 1806, from Book 1, p.62;

John Cumbow md. Polly Jennings on Aug. 19, 1794, from Book 1, p. 31.

Halifax County Bureau of Vital Statistics, LVA Reel 13:
1853, p.11, line 268- Char. C. Cumbee(hard to read), died at home in June, parents were Wm. H. and Elizabeth Cumbee, info provided by Wm. H. Cumbee, father;

1859, p. 51, line 27- Mary Cumbow, 57, white, died June 5, cause of death was chiles[sic], parents were D. and H. Cumby , born in Amelia, occupation was spinster, info provided by A. Cumboe, son.

1868, p. 103- Elizabeth E. Cumbie, died July, 1868, age 6 months, cause of death was unknown, father was Morgan Cumbie.

1873- (no first name) Halifax County Vital Statistics, births: William Cumbie was born on December 25, 1872. His parents were Edward and Martha Cumbie.

1870, line 16, Birch Creek Twnshp- Nancy Cumba, died June 12, 1870 from Typhoid fever, age was not given, parents were Solemon and Mary (perhaps May) Cumba, info provided by father.

1873- Amelia Cumby, white female, age 5, died of fever, parents were J.J. Cumbie and Camilla. Wm. J. Cumbie died 9/12/1873, at 6 months of age, from congestive chill, parents were J.J. and Camilla.
Cumby died at age of 3 days, cause unknown, parent was Sarah Cumby.

1882- Billie Comby died at age 30, from " dropsy heart ", info provided by husband John Comby.

1885- Ruth Cumby died on Dec.10, 1885, from heart disease, at age 80, consort of Alex Cumby, Wm and Polly Hughes were her parents.

From *HALIFAX COUNTY CEMETERIES VOL. 1*, p 284-
Buried at Oak Ridge Cemetery, corner of N. Main and Cavalier Blvd. in South Boston, VA-
Percy J.Cumby
s/o John R. and Beulah Cumby
b. 1896, d.1898;
John A. Cumby
s/o John R. and Beulah Cumby

b. 1902, d. 1904
Beulah Weatherford
w/o John R. Cumby
b. 1870, d. 1904;
John R. Cumby
b. 1857, d. 1948;
(Dee) Derilda Baynes
w/o John R. Cumby
b. 1868, d. 1946.
Buried at Dan River Baptist Church-
Morgan C. Cumbie
b. 9/20/1845, d. 10/11/1905.
Several other Cumby or Cumbie individuals are mentioned, including Camilla, George C.[Calvin], and others. Notes will be taken and added later as time permits.

Halifax County, General Index to Wills, Fiduciaries, Etc., 1752-1949-Pos.Reel 49 at the LVA-
1797-John Cumbo-Bk 3, p 316,
1808-Charles Cumbo-Bk 7, p.448,449,451,
1824-Elizabeth Cumbo-Bk13,p.305,
"   "   "   -Bk 14, 527,
1854-Thomas R. Combey-Bk24,p.2286,
1944-Blanche Comba –Bk 15,255.

From *MARRIAGES OF HALIFAX COUNTY, VIRGINIA: 1801-1831*-

Prudence H. Cumby married John R. Lester on 25 January 1830, Sur. Charles Cumby,

Martha Cumbie married Thompson Dunn on 25 December 1826,

Elizabeth Cumbo married Richard Dyer , 5 Aug 1807, signs her own consent,

18 Dec 1816 Charles Cumbie to Nancy Cornwall, md. On 22 Dec1816 by Rev. John Terry,

13 Jan 1819 William Cumbie and Elizabeth Powell, md on 14 Jan 1819 by Rev. David Street,

Alexander Cumb[o] married Mary Wilkerson on 9 Dec 1819,

1 June 1806 Peter Cumb[o] and Dolly Gray , wit. William Cumbo, md. Same day,

12 Jan 1804 Thomas Cumbo and Agnes Wetherford who signs her own consent.

From **General Index to Marriages Halifax Co. Va. Males-** Thomas Comba-Agnes Wetherford , Jan.12, 1804-Book 1, p.55,
Charles Combo-Elizabeth Maschiel, Sept. 7, 1786- Book 1, p. 9,
Peter Combo-Dolly Gray, June 1, 1806-Book 1, p.62,
John Cumbow-Polly Jennings, Aug. 19, 1794- Book 1, p. 31.

From *TYLER'S QUARTERLY HISTORICAL AND GENEALOGICAL MAGAZINE* (TQ),
"Marriage Bonds in Halifax County, VA"
1793-Ezekiel Mathews to S. Cumbo.

An email sent 10/7/2004:

"I went to the LVA yesterday to look for the Will of Charles Cumbo of Halifax Co., without success so far. Charles was probably a brother of Thomas Cumbo, Sr., who likely was our Thomas Cumby's father. I did find an inventory of Charles' estate, dated Dec. 10, 1802, and it is as follows: two feather beds and their furniture, ½ dozen earthen plates, 5 small bowls and one quart mug, 2 pewter [illegible] 4 plates and 2 dishes, 4 spoons & 2 small tin cups, 1 chist[sic] and table [very illegible], ½ dozen chairs, 1 [il., perhaps mare] saddle, 1 loom, 1 ole[sic] pot and hook and 1 ole oven, 6 ole hoes 1 cutter [Coulter?] 1 ole cotton wheel, 1 cooking glass, 1 ole pair of cotton & cards, 1 grinden [sic] stone, 1 pitcher and 1 flat [illegible], 1 pole ax, 3 head horses, 2 prs iron traces and collars, 11 head cattle, 15 head hogs, 6 forks and 5 knives, 1 water pail 1 piggin [?] & 1 tub. The inventory was very faded and in an odd handwriting, in other words, very hard to read. In 1824 Elizabeth Cumbo's estate was very similar. She was probably Charles' widow, the former Elizabeth Maschiel. I did notice that she owned a team of oxen. The plan is to keep looking for the Will that supposedly lists Charles and Elizabeth's children.

In the Halifax data at the LVA there are a great many mentions of Charles and Thomas Cumbo. Most of them do not add to our knowledge of the family tree. They consist largely of orders to work on clearing various roads in the County, payment of various taxes, lawsuits, etc. I am still reading the material, and I still hope to find useful sources."

An email sent 10/07/2004:

 The Will of Charles "Combo" is in Halifax County Will Book 6, p. 347. It reads as follows:

In the Lord one thousand Eight hundred & two March the Fourth day, I being in a low state of health but sound in mind & memory not knowing how soon it may please the Lord to

Call me from this State of life and feel myself desirous to dispose of my worldly goods as followeth[:] I give and bequeath to Dear beloving wife Elisbeth Combo all my kitching & household furniture also three Cows & calves one sorrel mare an[sic] a sorrel colt during her life or widowhood & my desire is that my land and the rest of my Stock be converted to the use of paying my debts, and if there should be more money arising from s. sale Transfer [illegeible word] it to my aforesaid Wife Elizabeth Combo & after her decease or marrying, my desire is that my daughter Lucy C. Combo Shall have ten pounds and an equal division with the rest of my children and an equal division to take place with the rest of my children, To wit, Molly, Sally, Elizabeth, Annis, Nancy, Elexander, William, Charles, & Lucy C. Combo, and I give to Nancy Maskill a Cow. This being my last will and Testament and assigned in the presence of Peter Ragland, William Drummond, Thomas Maskill, Richard Perkins.

Charles (his mark) Combo.

By April of 1802 Charles was deceased.

I have some comments on the above, which I will send later.

Another email sent on 10/17/2004:

"From page 348:

At a Court held for Halifax County the 25th day of April 1802 The within written Last Will and Testament of Charles Cumbo deceased was exhibited in Court and proved by the oaths of three of the Witnesses thereto Subscribed & ordered to be recorded. Teste John Wimbush CHC.

Charles Cumbo evidently died soon after making his Will. The Will was in probate for about six years. The signature X of Charles looks strange compared to other specimens that I have seen. Charles Cumbo had a very distinctive, personalized X, that is easy to remember, and the one on the Will is different. It looks rather like the mathematical symbol for "not equal to." Maybe somebody else noticed the difference two hundred years ago, and that may be why the Will was probated.

The Will below [above in these notes] indicates that the Charles Cumbo who made the Will was the same one who married Elizabeth "Maschiel" in 1786. Also, the guess that Maschiel was a variant spelling of Marshall seems disproved by the spelling below as Maskill, for it evidently was pronounced that way.

The Will of Charles Combo was not listed on the microfilm reel that purports to provide a complete index. I found it only because I happened by chance to notice it on a transcription. Now, if I can only find a similar document for Thomas and Susanna Cumbo, we should be able to say who our distant forebears were."

The Library of Virginia now has on microfilm a **GENERAL INDEX TO ORDER BOOKS (Halifax County), 1752-1900.**
This has almost six pages of orders relating to Cumbos and Cumbies. These orders have not been studied in detail to date (1/3/03), but an Order was noted that involved a Thomas Cumby, Jr., in 1773. This needs to be checked for accuracy, to be sure that it referred to Junior rather than to Senior.

Yesterday-Gone Forever, A Collection of Articles, by Faye Royster Tuck, includes "The Memoirs of LeGrand Michaux Jones", mentions Jones' seeing Elder John Weatherford at Mossingford Church in Charlotte County, in 1830 or 1831. Jones wrote that Weatherford "wore a knit woolen cap the whole time" that he was preaching. Blacks sat on the left of the church, separated from the whites by a railing. The church had a "large colored membership." Mrs. Tuck gave verbal permission for me to quote from her book, in a phone call on June 2, 2005.

Notes on Civil War Soldiers by WPA, from microfilm at the LVA-

Application for Admission to the Soldiers Home of R. E. Lee Camp No.1, Confederate Veterans, was made on March 8, 1927, by John H. Cumbea. He died on March 16, 1927 at 7 am. His nearest relative was Thomas J. Cumbea. J.H. Cumbea's birth date was given as Oct. 5, 1851. He enlisted as Private in 1861, C Co 21 st Va Inf, discharged at end of war. He was color bearer, paroled at Appomattox. Appended is a statement: "I Marvin Nuckols certify that the applicant John H. Cumbea is of sound mind, and not an habitual drunkard, nor has he ever been an inmate of an insane asylum." His nearest relative was identified as Thomas J. [Jonathon] Cumbea.

THE VIRGINIA REGIMENTAL HISTORIES SERIES, found at the LVA, provided the names of the military units in which numerous individuals served. Using those unit identifications, I was able to find WPA notes for individuals of interest to the Cumbia family.

WPA notes on John H. Cumby-
He enlisted on June 28, 1861.Was marked absent because taken prisoner at Kerrstown.
Another entry gives the date of enlistment as June 20, 1861, [? different from above], gives place of enlistment as Christiansville.
In various entries his name is spelled Cumby, Cumbey, and Cumbea.
On Feb. 20, 1862, he was furloughed for 25 days (another entry gives 30 days).
On March 23, 1862, he was listed as missing, was captured at Winchester on 3/23/1862.

On Oct. 19, 1864 [the entry was made on Oct. 31] John was an Ensign and had the 3rd and 4th fingers of his left hand amputated due to shell wound, "at carpophalangeal articulation."

Ensign and 1st Lieutenant, applied for retirement on April 20, 1864. He was advised to remain on duty.

WPA Notes -W. E. Cumbie, almost certainly Robert Allen Cumbia's older brother called Willie, enlisted in the Confederate Army on January 20, 1862 in Mecklenburg County, for "War." Willie served in the VA Inf. 22nd Bn Co D, also in the 21st Inf. Co. F. Willie died on May 24 or 26, 1864 (both dates appear in the WPA notes), in the General Hospital at Staunton, from " Vulnus Sclopeticum " (gunshot wounds) received at the Battle of the Wilderness.

I checked the **Staunton Vindicator** at the LVA, hoping to find some mention of the death of Willie Cumbie, but his death was not mentioned. In the edition of May 13, 1864 I found the following:

"For the past few days large numbers of those wounded in the late fights have arrived at Stauntion. They were met at the trains by many of the Ladies of this place, who supplied them with various little delicacies prepared for them. Our hospital is full of these gallant unfortunates, who have been wounded in defending our homes and firesides from the ruthless invader, and while we cannot heal their wounds by a simple wish, we can ameliorate their condition much by sending many little things not generally needed for family use, which will be thankfully received by them.

The attention of the Country people is especially directed to this patriotic and humane duty. Send to the wounded any thing you can spare and send at once."

An incarcerated youth at RDC suggested that I might find Willie's grave at **Thorne-Rose Cemetery in Staunton**. The youth was from Staunton and knew that the Cemetery was both very old and very large. I phoned Thorne-Rose, and I learned that no one named Willie Cumbie was known to be buried there. I was told that about 700 Confederate soldiers were buried in a mass grave and that it was very likely that Robert Allen's brother lies buried among them. That so many soldiers had to be buried in such a short time made it impossible for good records to be kept, so we may never know for sure.

Emily F. Cumbee [sic] applied for a pension on April 27, 1909. Her deceased husband was James Lewis Cumbea, who had been a member of Co C 21st Va Regiment, officer was Capt. A. J. Hayes. James died on April 10, 1899, of consumption. Emily stated that she lived with "our in laws." She claimed $ 25 worth of personal property. James served in the CSA Army from 1861 –1865. His captain wrote that he was a brave soldicr.

WPA Notes on James L. Cumbea-
James enrolled on June 20, 1861, at Christiansville, by Capt. Oliver. He was mustered into service on June 22, 1861 in Richmond, VA, by Gen. Baldwin, enlisted for one year. Absent, in hospital at Staunton, VA, Nov., Dec., 1861, according to record dated 12/31/ 1861.
Oct. 31, 1862, detailed as ambulance driver.
February 28, 1863, detailed as teamster.
James appears on a report of casualties in Battle of Winchester, March 23, 1862, "slightly wounded."
In various entries, James surname is spelled Cumby, Cumbya, Cumbea, and Cumbia.
James served in the VA 21st Inf. Co. C.

Robert W. Cumby served in the 18th VA Infantry. He was from Campbell County. He died at division hospital on July 20, 1864.

Edward Green Cumby enlisted on May 18, 1861, at Boydton, VA. He was a private in the 38th Infantry, Co. G. He was present until listed as deserted on July 22, 1862, returning on May 1, 1863. Again he was listed as deserted in February, 1865, but he returned in time to be a POW at Amelia CH on April 5, 1865. He was sent to City Point and then to Point Lookout on April 13, 1865. He was released at Point Lookout on June 10, 1865. He was a resident of Mecklenburg County, with dark complexion, brown hair and grey eyes, 5'8 ¼ inches tall.

James Pritchard from Mecklenburg County served in the VA 11th Infantry Co. D. He enlisted on March 1, 1862. He was absent due to sickness from January 1863 until he died on April 5, 1863 of pneumonia in Petersburg, VA. He was buried in a mass grave at Blandford Cemetery in Petersburg. I believe that this person was the husband of Catherine Cumby Pritchard.

Z. W. Curtis, an ancestor of Carolyn Davis, was wounded on July 3, 1863, at the Battle of Gettysburg, and he was also wounded at Drewrys Bluff, "hit halfway between knee and hip."

Thomas Cumby, Jr., served in the 18th Infantry. $75.23 in back pay was sent to his father at Evergreen P.O. in Appomattox County. Thomas was killed at the Battle of Sharpsburg on September 17, 1862. He had enlisted on March 1, 1862, for three years. [This individual, in spite of his name, does not seem to have been a brother of George and Major.]

Thomas S. Cumby enlisted in Prince Edward County. He was captured at Harper's Farm on April 6, 1865, sent to City Point, VA on April 14, then released on June 26, 1865, after taking the oath of allegiance. He was described as being 5'8" tall.

The following is an email that I sent to interested family members:

"This morning at the LVA I found the Confederate service records and the pension applications of Alexander Griffith, Mary Cumbia's father, and Paschal Cabiness, Ann Cumbia's husband.

P.Y.Cabiness applied for a pension on April 24, 1908. He was 72 years old, and he lived in Chase City at the time. He stated that he was born in Lunenburg County. He had lived at his present address for 47 years. He said he was a carpenter and had been one all his life. He gave as the cause of his disability " hard work and old age." The nature of his disability was "deafness, bodily infirmities and old age." He said he was in the army for 3 years and left service "In 1865, was at Surrender." His signature is on the app!

The service record of P.Y.Cabiness shows him almost always present. He served as a Private in the VA 34th Infantry Co. B. He was detailed as a cook in 1864. He was admitted to Chimborazo Hospital No.6 on June 21, 1864. On July 17, 1864 his officer, Capt. T.T. Pettits [illegible] wrote a "request for 15 day furlough to visit his family in Mecklenburg County" and added that he was a "deserving and faithful soldier" and "that he has not violated nor failed to report the violation of any known order within the last sixty days."

"**Alexander Griffith** (also called Griffis) applied for a pension on October 24, 1904. He said he had served in the 3rd VA Cavalry, Fitzhugh Lee's Division, Army of Northern Virginia, Co. A. He stated that he was disabled due to "spinal trouble caused by horse falling with me a[t] Winchester." He stated that he had lived at his present address of South Hill for 60 years. He was a farmer for 25 years, and during the previous 2 years had "Kept a mill, Got $95 per year." While in service he suffered "a spell of Typhoid fever." He said he "can do but little, sometimes can do nothing." The application has Griffith's mark, an X."

"Alexander Griffith enlisted at Boydton onJuly 25, 1861 for one year. He was called a teamster and a wagon driver. He was sick at home in January, 1862. He was at Chimborazo Hospital No.1 on August 2, 1862. He was captured on July 5, 1863 near Wmsport, Md. He was admitted to the USA General Hospital at Chester, PA on July 14, 1863, then transferred to City Point (present day Hopewell) on September 17, 1863. Present at Yorktown on April 1, 1864, he was absent May and June 1864 because "detailed to procure fresh horse." He was at Appomattox C.H. at the surrender. Alexander Grifffith was also called Alex and N.A. Mary's father's name was Nathaniel Alexander."

"Today's trip to the Library was well worth the trouble."

Appomattox County, Virginia

The following email was sent to the cousins:

This will be something most of you have seen before, but I wanted to type it up to add it to my compiled notes, and I wanted to email it again, for those who missed it the first time.

The following was an article published in the local (Lawrenceville, VA) newspaper:

"The War Record of John H. Cumbea, 1st Lieutenant, 21st Regiment, 2nd Brigade, Jackson's Old Division, Army of Northern Virginia

As Told By Himself After His 80th Birthday-10-8-1841, 3-?-1927

Will give you a little of my experience and close calls of the Civil War times.

I joined the Confederate Army in June, 1861. The first of my fighting was at Kerrstown in March, 1862[,] where I was taken prisoner and carried to Fort Delaware. I remained there until after the seven days battle around Richmond. We had short rations besides being cooked with little regard to cleanliness. The beef soup and rice was often thickened with young green flies, but we had to eat it or go without anything. The water we had for drinking was hauled there by boat load and dumped on shore in barrels and lay in the sun for weeks at a time.

I was exchanged in August, 1862[,] and I went to my company while they were in Frederick City, Maryland. There my fighting commenced. I was in the battles thus mentioned: Harper's Ferry, Fredericksburg, Chancellorsville, Wilderness, Spotsylvania C.H. and down to Richmond. Returned to the valley of Virginia again by Lynchburg to the mountains. From there to Frederick City, Maryland, again had battle at the Monocacy River, from there to the near approach of Washington City, causing much consternation among the Cabinet of the Federals.

The next big battle I was in was Gettysburg, Pennsylvania, then Winchester, Goshens Hill, Cedar Creek near Winchester, where I got my hand partly shot off while carrying the colors. I forgot to mention that the closest call of my time was at Fisher[']s Hill where the enemy flanked us. The whole left wing of the regiment fell back. I was in the center with my colors and guard. We held our ground with the right wing of the regiment until the enemy was within 40 feet of us. As I started to run I dashed from under my hat and did not have time to pick it up without being captured with my colors. As I ran I tore them off the staff to keep from being such a desirable target for them. Out of the 8 guards that went with the colors, only two ran out with me, and one of them was killed before he got a hundred yards. Now, all of you, old soldiers, can imagine what kind of color bearer I looked like with the flag in my bosom and the staff in my hand, running back to a place a little more desirable for the formation of the line again.

When my hand got well from the wound I received at Cedar Creek I returned to my regiment at Petersburg, Virginia, took part in the battle of Hatcher's Run in February, 1865, and then from Petersburg to Appomattox. There I tore my colors up in strips and gave some of it to the few of us that were present rather than deliver it up to the victor."

At first I thought the above was probably an old man's harmless bragging, but examining numerous records of John Cumbea's service has changed my mind. He was where he was when he said he was there, and he was wounded when and where he said. He was held as a POW. He was a color bearer. Although he enlisted as a private, he was eventually promoted to Lt. I tend now to believe the old man, and I think he may have been the source of the often told story of the colors being torn and divided at Appomattox. He was the one who tore them.

Best wishes from Sam

Bureau of Vital Statistics, Appomattox County, from microfilm at the Library of Virginia-

William Cumbio married Mary Ida Smith on Dec. 8, 1886. She was 22, and he was 24. WC was from Campbell County, and his parents were Wm. S. Cumbio (perhaps Cumbia) and ?

Major T. Cumby married Lucy Woolridge on Dec. 27, 1886. He was 22, she was 21. Neither had been married before. He was born in Richmond, VA. His parents were "decd." Wife's father was Daniel Woolridge.

J.J. Cumby, a farmer, married Lizzy P. Martin on April 23, 1887. He was born in Charlotte County. She was from Appomattox. His parents were Jno Cumby and wife. Hers were William A. Martin and wife.

J.T. Cumby, a farmer, married Elnora V. Martin on June 29, 1892.His parents were J.J. Cumby and wife. Her parents were P.D. Martin and wife.

Nannie S. Cumby, 14, married Lorenzo [very hard to read] D. Williams, 22, on May 12, 1895. Her father was Saml H. Cumby.

Elvira Cumby, 22, married T. H. Tolley, 22, on August 13, 1895. She was born in Appomattox County. Her father was Thos. S. Cumby.

Walter Cumby, 23, married Mary Randolph, 28, on December 7, 1898. He was single, she was divorced. His father was Peter Cumby, hers was John Cumby. He was born in Campbell County , she was born in Appomattox County.

Saml. H. Cumby, 22, a farmer, married Ossie Mitchell, 22, on July 2, 1881. Saml's parents were S. Cumby and wife.

Bureau of Vital Statistics, Appomattox County, deaths-
July 10, 1861- Wm. T. Cumby, WM, died, cause unknown, 9years old, parents were Wm. S. and Sarah M. Cumby, born in Appomattox Co. info from father;

--1862-Eliza Cumby died, of consumption, 50 years old, born in Campbell, wife of Thomas Cumby;

April 24, 1864- Illegible [possibly Ann or Amy] Cumby died, from pneumonia, 77 years old, parents were Martin and Mary Logan, born in Charlotte Co., wife of Simeon Cumby;

July 2, 1865-Frank A. Cumby died , from flu, age 25, parents were Thomas and E. Cumbie, born in Campbell, Susan Cumbey was his wife- record was very hard to read;

--1865-Rebecca Coleman died, age 27, parents were Simeon and Ann Cumby, born in Halifax Co.;

June 30, 1878, Martha Cumby, WF, died from pneumonia, at her father's residence, age 11, Jno Cumby and wife were parents.

1860 Census of Appomattox Co.-
Simeon Cumby, p. 497, Tower Hill P.O. – I did not find and transcribe these records yet.

1870 Census of Appomattox Co.-
Dwel, Fam. 218-
Cumby, John J.-25- laborer on farm
"   , Elizabeth-35-keeps house
"   , Saml H.   11

"   , John   9
"   , Martha A.   3

Dwel,Fam, 224-
Cumby, Thomas - 67-farm laborer
"   , Martha - 23- keeps house
"   , Eliza   - 20
"   , Peter   - 21 - farm laborer
"   , Martha S. - 9.

I checked the **Chesterfield County Vital Statistics**, Register of Births for 1883-1895, but I found no Cumbys.

The 1880 Census of Brunswick County, VA, Sturgeon Magisterial District, Page 30-

Cumbia, John H.,   38;
"   , Winnifred, 36;
"   , Laura,   13;
"   , Charles H., 12;
"   , Grace,   10;
"   , William,   8;
"   , Thomas,   7;
"   , Harriet E., 5;
"   , Minnie,   4;
"   , Viola,   2;
"   , Annie,   2/12, May.

The 1910 Census of Brunswick County, VA, Powellton District,

Family, Dwelling # 64-
Cumbia, C.H., 42, Head [Charles Henry],
"   , F.A., 46, Wife [Florence Flint Cumbia],
"   , J.A. , 12, Son,
"   , F.M., 8, Dtr. [illegible],
"   , H.D., 6, Son,
"   , J.H. , 68 [Charles' father, John Henry].

1910 Census of Brunswick County, VA, Lawrenceville District, Family, Dwelling #173-

Cumbia, Willie,   37[William Allen];
"   , Mattie,   32[Mattie Abernathy];
"   , Winnifred, 12;
"   , Willie M.,   10 [Marvin, ran a store at Cochran, VA];
"   , Harriet R., 6;
"   , Edward N., 2.[Norfleet Cumbia];
"   , " "   , Mary S. , 1/12.

1900 Census of Brunswick County-Family and Dwelling # 124-

R.A.Cumbia, M.A.[Mary Allen Griffith Cumbia, called Mollie] , Mami, C.A.[Charles Allen, called Charlie],A.B [Anna Bell, called Sue].,R.I [Robert Ivan, called Ivan].,Deseri [called Dessie],Otis A.,G.B.[George Burnice, called Burnice],Clarence [Clarence David, usually called David]. Ages were not recorded. The Brunswick County residence confirms the recollections of Oscar Cumbia's friend Emmit Pulley.

The **Death Certificate of John H. Cumbia** names his father as George Cumbia and the birthplace of his father as Campbell County. His mother was Pamelia Anne Wells. He was the widower of Winifred Thompson. He died on March 16, 1927. His birth date was July 13, 1841. He died due to Valvulor [sic] Disease of Heart& Arteriosclerosis. He was buried in Oakwood Cemetery in Richmond. [off Nine Mile Rd.]

 Civil War Soldiers from Brunswick County, Virginia, by Pritchett and Pritchett has a chapter on John Henry Cumbia. Although it is gratifying to see John getting recognition for his service, the book unfortunately repeats Dorothy's understandable mistake regarding the identities of John's parents, and it lists Anna Belle (Aunt Sue) among John's children. She was a daughter of Robert Allen and Mary Cumbia.

Brunswick County Marriage Book 1, p. 87, line 2, records the marriage of John Cumby to Winifred R. Thompson on Feb. 22, 1866. James and Martha Cumby were listed as John's parents, which is almost certainly, given much other evidence, incorrect. Charles and Winifred Thompson were listed as her parents.

Julia Cumbea, Mrs. Fred Cumbea, provided the following information about the family and descendants of James and Emily's son, John Robert.

James Lewis and Emily Crow Cumbea's son John Robert Cumbea b.Jan.22,1879 d.Aug.26,1953.Born in Mecklenburg County. Married Sallie Ann Connell or Conner in Brunswick County in 1901.Sallie b.Aug.30,1878 d.Jan.7,1969.Both are buried in Maury Cemetary in Richmond,Va.
They had 11 children all born in Mecklenburg County.Most of info. came from family members and I to cemetaries to verify dates of birth and death.

1Clyde Davis Cumbea b.march1902 d.Dec.7, 1985
married Irvine William Taylor Dec.3,1919
I.W.Taylor b.1892 d.1953.He served in W.W.1.
        They had 5 girls
Ruby b.sept.14,1920 in Mecklenburg Co.
Dorothy b.Feb.18,1924 Mecklenburg Co.
Jessie Mae b.April20,1925 d.Feb.1997 Mecklenburg Co.
ANNE b.Sept.24,1932 Chesterfield Co.
Barbara Lee b.June 2,1941 d.Mar.10,2002 born in Chesterfield Co. died in Gates CO.N.C.

#2John Lewis Cumbia b.oct.28, 1904 d.July 25,1987. John had a twin to die at birth;
married Catherine Price Harris April 28,1945;
Catherine b.april28,1923.
John is buried at Independence Christian Church in Hanover
They had 2 children
Mary Ann b. sept.17, 1947 d.aug.31, 1963 in auto accident.

Catherine Ann, b.oct.18, 1964, married Dale Fetty Dec.16, 2000.

#3 Nettie B.b.sept.7,1907 d.dec.12,1996.Buried at Maury Cemetery;
married Joseph William Gay dec.12,1928.
2 children
John Wilber, b.oct.21,1929, d.feb.1,1956 accident. Buried at Maury Cemetary
Bettie b.march13,1931.

#4Russell Rawlings b.sept.5,1908 d.aug.8,1959. Buried at Maury Cemetary; married Grace Odell Godsey Feb 19, 1930 in Chesterfield CO.
Grace b.July 4,1914, had 5 children:
Dolores W., b.june9,1931;
Russell R. jr. b..JULY 17, 1933   [was a twin Grace lost when she was 4.5 months];
Frederick L. b.april 20,1940;
Laraine J. b.Jan.7,1943;
Ken E. b.oct.19,1947;

#5 Walter Swanson,b. JULY17, 1911, d.aug.6, 1977. Buried at Maury Cemetery.He was a Private in U.S.Army.
[sorry but I have not been able to get dates on his marriages or children yet will get back with you later.] He was married 4 times.
     #1.Ellen Godsey -no children;
     #2.Velma [they had 3 children]:
          1.Walter W.
          2.Beverly
          3.Janice
     #3 Janie   [married her 2 times so that is the 4th marriage;

#6 Ethel Catherine b.June 10 1913[The only living child of John and Sallie she is in a nursing home] Married 3 times:
1.Fredrick Henson Francis-1 child-Mary Ann b.nov.28,1930;
2.Wesley Wyatts-no children-He adopted Mary Ann;
3.John Crowder;

7 William Edward b.June 8,1915 d.April 16,1999. Buried at Dale Memorial in chesterfield,county,

married Ellen Nunnally,
Ellen b.June 14,1908 d.Jan.24,1999
[Ed and Ellen had no children together];

8Woodrow Wilson b.oct.17,1917 d.nov.6,2000.Buried at Maury Cemetary;
Married 3 times:
1. Ruby Hicks , April 12,1943
b.Nov.4,1920 d.June,1979. Buried at maury cemetary
2 children;
1.Herbert W.b.Jan.29,1943;
2.Linda Gail b.sept.10,1946;
2.Nannie Stevenson b.mar1,1918 d.mar.22,1992;
3.Eva Bell Hardee b.feb.27,1930 d.nov.16,1993;

9 GILBERT Andrew b.oct.25 d.sept.29,1994.Buried at Maury Cemetary
W.W.11 VETEREN
Married 3 times:
1.Ivy Sampson met and married in Dorset England April 24 ,1942;
Ivy b.Jan.11,1924 (England)
2 children:
1.Velma Ballard b.nov.8,1944 in England;
2.Margaret Faye b.nov.17,1946;

2.Margarette ?;

3.Grace Godsey Cumbea (married brothers);

#10 Robert Lee Cumbea b.mar.18,1922

d.sept.22,1990.Buried in Maury Cemetary;

Robert was in w.w.11.He was Major at Richmond City Jail-RICHMOND, Va.;

> Married Nettie Hicks Jan.11,1946
>> Nettie b.Jan.22,1923
> 4 children

1.Robert Lee b.Dec.12,1946 d.Aug.14,1961 (drowned);

2.Phyllis Marie b.Mar.21,1948;

3.Raymond Barney b,NOV.10,1951;

4.Deborah Ann b.oct.6,1962.

Bureau of Vital Statistics, Brunswick County-

Recorded the death in 1896 of an unnamed Cumbia infant, the child of C. H. and [illegible, looks like F.A.] Cumbia, lived only one day. [C.H. was Charles Henry, and his wife Florence was F.A.]

Brunswick County Index to Marriage Registers- 1850 – 1948

John Cumby married. Winefred R. Thompson on February 22, 1866, recorded in Bk. 1, p. 87, l. 2.

Charles Henry Cumbia (son of John Cumbia)md. Florence Flint on October 9, 1895,

John Robert Cumbia (23) married Sallie A. Connell (22) on January 22, 1901. John's parents were Jas & E.F. Cumbia.

1910 Census of Brunswick County, Powellton District-

Fam., Dwelling 64-

Cumbia, C.H.,	42, Head [Charles Henry];	
" , F.A.,	46, Wife [Florence Flint];	
" , J. A.,	12, Son [John Albert];	
" , F. M.,	8, Dtr. [Name is illegible];	
" , H. D.,	6, Son [Henry];	

"   , J. H.   68 [Relationship was not identified, but this was John Henry, the father of Charles Henry.]

Fam., Dwelling 173-
Cumbia, Willie,   37;
"   , Mattie R.,   32;
"   , Winnifred,   12;
"   , Willie M.,   10[Marvin];
"   , Harriett R.,   6;
"   , Edward N.,   2[Norfleet];
"   , Mary S.,   1/12.

Bureau of Vital Statistics, Brunswick County-
1896-Cumbia, not named, child of C.H. and F.A. Cumbia, lived one day.

Gaye Neal's history of Brunswick County mentions that George B. Cumbia [Burnice] and Edward Marshall Cumbia were veterans of World War 1.

Prince George County, Virginia-

1850 Census of Prince George County, on microfilm at the
Library of Virginia-
Major Cumbia , 37, M, Overseer,
Elizabeth " , 31, F,
John " , 14, M,
Thomas " , 12, M,
Mary " , 10, F,
William " , 7.

1860 Census of Prince George County, on microfilm at the
Library of Virginia-
Family no. 542-
M. W. Cumby, [Major Weatherford], 45, M, farmer, RE
3000, PE 4000,
N. B. Cumby, 50, F, [the N is hard to read, looks like an A,
but evidently this is Nancy B. Morgan Cumby]
J. N. 24, M, [Major and Nancy's son John]
T. H. 22, M, [Thomas]
W. A. 15, M. [William].

The 1860 Slave Schedule of Prince George County, VA,
on p. 44,
identifies M.W.Cumbia as owner of the following: one black
male, 55; one black female, 18; one black male, 17; one
black male, 2; and one black male, 1.

1870 Census of Prince George County, on microfilm at the
Library of Virginia-
Major Cumbia [or Cumbea], 58, M, farmer,
Delia " , 38, F, keeping house,
M.J.C. " , 8, M,

Infant,   "   , 1 mo., M, born in May,
     "   "   "   "   "'
William C. Webb, 19, M, attending school,
Sarah Hobbs, 26, F, domestic servant.

The 1870 Census of Chesterfield County reported a John Cumby, a black roofer, aged 70, living in Dale Township. He lived with a black woman named Sophia, 75. John Cumby may have been the older male slave that Major owned in 1860.

The 1870 Census of Prince George County listed a Nancy Comby, white female, in dwelling 252 and family 253, in the household of Emaline Cox. This person seems to have been too old to have been Major's first wife.

From a letter by Dr. William Scarborough of the University of Southern Mississippi to Mrs. J. Major Cumbea, dated October 9, 1967, found in Dorothy Cumbea's notes– "Cumbea managed White Hill Plantation [which belonged to Charles Friend], located two miles east of Petersburg on City Point Road in Prince George County, Virginia during the period 1846-1858." He managed the labor of about 65 slaves, growing mainly wheat and corn. He did some carpentry work, and he sometimes managed the farm for long periods in the absence of Mr. Friend.

Dr. Scarborough wrote a book called *The Overseer*. He devoted about a page to Major Weatherford Cumbea, who he called a good example of an ambitious, upwardly mobile person. Dr. Scarborough described the life of the overseer as a hard, often lonely one. Socially, an overseer was considered to be beneath the family of the plantation owner, and he was seldom permitted to socialize with them. He often was not allowed to have his own family live on the plantation with him, nor was he permitted to socialize with the slaves. An overseer would usually have a small dwelling on the plantation grounds, perhaps with the services of a slave or slaves. He would be expected to work all day and to be on call at all times. He would usually have a contract for a year's work, but sometimes other arrangements were made, including the option of immediate dismissal at the will of the master. Dr. Scarborough thought that Major was a bachelor during his employment at White Hill. Although Major was married to Nancy while he worked for Friend, it is likely that they lived apart for long periods of time.

Prince George County Marriage Register, on microfilm at the LVA-
M.W.Cumbea married Adelia Hobbs on Oct. 24, 1860. He was 47, she was 25. He was a widower, she was single. His birthplace was Charlotte County, and his parents were "Thos & A Cumbea." The marriage was performed by A. Stuart. The groom was a farmer. Their residence was Prince George County.

From records at the Prince George County Courthouse-
Cumbea, M.W., Estate of, Prince George, 1873 entry,
58 acres, near Petersburg, bearing NW from the C. H., distance-7 miles, Total value of land per acre, including buildings – 30, sum included in the value of each tract of land on account of buildings – 100, total value of land and buildings 1,740.
1872 entry-mentions "water courses near which it [Major's land] lies" – Appomattox River. Using a current map, with a scale, one can see that Major's farm probably was in the vicinity of the gravel pits owned and dug by Vulcan. The gravel pits are on both sides of Temple Ave, between Hopewell and Colonial Heights.

From an email on May 15, 2003, re. Papers, 1792-1871 1839-1871), The diaries and account book of Charles Friend, Call Number Mss 1 F9156 at the Virginia Historical Society-

"This morning I visited the Virginia Historical Society, which has the original records of White Hill Plantation. I began to study the Diary of Charles Friend . It contains numerous references to Major Weatherford Cumbea. Although I saw only a small part of the records, the following notes were taken:

December 25, 1845 - " Christmas and all hands enjoying the Holy days...It snowed a little on the 26th."

Dec. 30 - " Commenced work again the Holy days having gone off very quietly - Jack and Peter moving Mr. Cumby-Ned and the women opening the furrows where ever the water stood on the wheat."

December 31, 1845 - "Jack and Peter moving Mr. Cumby- Lo ends the year, and a very happy one it has been, tho not very bountiful and all we need is thankfulness for the many blessings which have crowned the year and confidence in believing that all the events of the next will be for our good if our hearts are given to God. "Amen" "

January 1, 1846, Thursday - "Jack and Peter went to the forest for Mr. Cumbea's furniture."

A slave ran away, returned on his own, was whipped.

Mr. Friend returned from an absence and wrote that, given the bad weather and sickness among the slaves, his overseer had performed very well.

From 1851-

March 3rd -" Commenced seeding oats. Five shovel and two turn ploughs getting them in-Mr. Cumbea seeding."
March 15th -"...Jim ploughed Mr. Cumbea's garden.
April 2nd - "Mr. Cumbea spaid the Hogs this morning."
April 5th - "Mr. Gibson [minister] dined with us and preached to the servants in the evening. May the Lord bless his Labour."
April 12th - mention of "Dr. Withers, Dr. Broadnax, Mr. Atkinson Broadnax" [My boyhood home was Brodnax]
April 22 - " Albert was hauling wood to Mr. Cumbea's house and to the kitchen."
April 24th - mention of " Fodder and some wood to Mr.Cumbea's house."
June 27 - "Penda [slave] lost her child [due to] convulsions.
June 28 - " We lost some time by the Funeral Services of Penda's child at which Mr. Gibson officiated....Mr. Cumbea absent. The hottest day this year.

From an email sent on 8/8/2003:

"Yesterday afternoon I took more notes on the Charles Friend Diaries, too many to send them all now, but I want to pass along some of the more interesting parts. I was primarily interested in any mention of M.W.Cumbea but also in the treatment of the slaves. I read the 1858 entries to see what Friend would say about Cumbea's departure.

From 1850-

Oct. 12-Albert hauled a load of wood to Mr. Cumbea's and to the kitchen with the oxen....Henry had leave of absence on account of the death of his wife and Jim took his place.

Nov. 2- ... wood to Mr. Cumbea's...My mule Fillice died, from distemper and old age- she has been working on this farm since eighteen hundred and thirty four- no great loss.[Earlier, Mr. Friend had written how his mules were really not strong enough to do good work on his plantation.] One of my neighbor's hogs was killed on this farm by Albert- who was sent to drive it out and at night taken by John and Henry to eat or sell- The party flogged- and I am ready to pay for the hog as soon as the owner is assortained[sic].

Nov. 3- ...repaired fence around Mr. Cumbea's house and garden.

Nov. 7- Molly came home this morning after an absence of more than five months. She is so far gone in pregnancy that I fear to have her whipped so I shall have to postpond[sic] that disagreeable duty to a later period.

1857-

Feb.1-...wood to Mr. Cumbea's....[Friend wrote with evident worry about what an unusually cold spell they had, with deep snow and temperatures as low as 6 degrees F. The slaves were digging out the paths and the road.]

Apr. 20- ... the men with Mr. Cumbea about tobacco....

May 6...[mentions]Mary Jane who is washing for Mr. Cumbea....

1850-

July 11-Commenced threshing wheat after much difficulty in getting it [
the threshing machine, which broke down and which they had difficulty getting a mechanic to repair] to work- and Mr. Cumbea had to fix it at last.

1858-

Apr. 11- My overseer has been very ill all the week past and is yet so-we had rain at night.

Apr. 19-The hands did not work until breakfast my overseer being sick.

July 2- All hands worming tobacco which we find most seriously injured by the worms, and my overseer who was raised in Tobacco says he never saw it so much eaten or so many worms at this season of the year.

Nov. 1- All my team are engaged in getting in wheat for Mr. Cumbea on the place he has purchased.

Dec. 12-The Ploughmen at work- the ox carts and Tumbrels [are] moving Mr.Cumbea to a farm he has bought in the neighborhood. He has been living with me thirteen years.

Dec. 14- [mentions] Mr. Clayton who takes Mr. Cumbea's place....

There are many more notes, but they are primarily mentions of mundane details such as wood being hauled to Mr. Cumbea's, etc.

Best wishes to all from Sam"

From **Section 3 Diary of Charles Friend 1851-1860**
August 22 - "Four men at work on Mr. Cumbea's kitchen." A slave named Ellick was whipped for being found sleeping when he was supposed to be working. August 26 - kitchen completed.
September 30 " This Journal has been kept by my Overseer during my absence at the White Sulfur from the 27th of August and copied in this book by myself."
November 28th - "Mr. Cumbea discovered a small bag Corn hid in the wagon of straw going to town. Henry White being the Driver I had him flogged and he said

Charles put it in his wagon. Charles being flogged confessed the deed - and I hope we have no more of it." December 2 - chicken pox, " through the family black & white."

Let me just mention, given that I saw in a very large number of pages two whippings documented, that almost every page details the condition of the slaves, were they well or sick and the treatment that they received. Almost every page indicates that slaves were not worked due to illness or pregnancy or that they were given light duty inside the house. They had holy days off, and religious services, including at least one funeral, were arranged for them.

Mr. Friend tended to end each year's entries with some spiritual interpretation of the events, including an expression of gratitude."

The notes that follow were taken from the **Diary** of Charles Friend, Section 2, 1847-1850, at the Historical Society of Virginia. Mr. Cumbea was Major Weatherford Cumbea, Friend's overseer.

"and thus ends the journal for another year-happy-happy year. ye are gone, and I pray that I may be dealt mercifully with when I come to give in my account of the Deeds done during their Lapse and oh that the next two may pass away as sweatly and peaceful."

1847-

July 14 - "sometime since my barn was broken into and I had an examination into the matter which resulted in the conviction of Jack, Joe, Henry[and]John-all of whom were soundly whipped and I have sent Joe to jail to be sold as he has been engaged in several misdemeanors before and was found having a secret key to the barn."

July 15 - "Jack who was whipped for stealing corn out my barn was reported as having been seen around my house every night since this punishment so I sent him to be sold this evening."

End of 1847-"Thus ends the year [,] its pleasures and its cares-and although I have had my perplexities-the year has been crowned with blessings far -very- far beyond my deserts and I have nothing but thanks to render and prayers that the next may prove as happy and , abundant, fare-well, old year."

1848-

Feb. 18-"...Jim [is] assisting Mr. Cumbea in seeding clover seed."

Feb. 23 - "Armistead [is] assisting Mr. Cumbea in building a mule stable."

April - Armistead and Jim with Mr. Cumbea [are] build[ing] stable.

May 29 - "Sunday" "John who was flogged on Saturday took himself off and has not returned- no one of my servant[s] can be corrected by an overseer that does not run off [without running away]- so much for having a town [Petersburg] near."

1849 -

Jan. 3 - "....brought down hogs for Mr. Cumbea."

Feb. 20 - "Agnis [is] with Penda [.] Jim went for a midwife...."

Feb. 21 - "Penda had a baby about 10 o'clock- Aggy & Molly [were] with the midwife."

Feb. 27 - "Lost two calves last night....Mary [a slave? Mrs. Friend? I don't know] brought forth a fine boy this morning[.]Jim went for and carried Midwife back to town -cold and drizly all day."

March 30 - "The journal for these four months preceding was kept by my overseer while I was in Alabama, it is quite minute and does him great credit as it is the first he thus ever kept in his life."

On another occasion, Friend returned and wrote about what a great job his overseer had done; then he added later that some of the work had not been as good as he had first believed.

Apr. 14 - mentions " the overseer's house."

May 18 - "Albert ... [is] working on Mr. Cumbea's garden."

May 19 - "I gave the hands the day to clean out their houses which I had white washed inside and hope to do so outside very soon[.] this I hope will tend to the preservation of the health of the Negroes."

July 5 - "Mr. Cumbea [is] seeding peas brought before the ploughs."

July 6 - "Ellick who was slap[p]ed for not being at the stable in time this morning took himself off."

July 7 - " ...Ellick made his appearance last night [.] I put him to weeding this morning but on Mr. Cumbea's attempt to flog him for this rebellion on yesterday - rebelled again to day and very harsh means had to be used with him before he could be subdued [,] which was accomplished however and he was soundly whip[p]ed for it....

Mr. Gibson preached this evening and they buried Penda's infant which died last night - My large sow had pigs yesterday....Ellick [was] ...whipped again yesterday."

I should add that almost every page, 70 of which I read, contains some expression of concern about the health of various slaves. Slaves were " in the house" when injured or ill. Friend several times remarked on the unusual state that found everyone well enough to work. Rev. Gibson held religious services for the slaves.

I will also mention that hauling things, especially manure, took up a tremendous amount of time and labor. Manure was, to my surprise, usually brought to the farm from town. Evidently it was produced by the horses of townfolk with little need for its fertilizing properties.

When the weather was bad, everyone worked inside. Holy days were usually days off.

At the funeral of a slave, one of the mourners said that Mr. Friend had been more like a father than a master to the slave. [no comment]

The above slave named Ellick continued to live and work on the Friend plantation.

From an email sent on 1/15/2005:

This morning I went to Battlefield Park at Petersburg, in order to look at some papers related to the Friend family and White Hill Plantation. The main thing I wanted to see – and saw- was a pamphlet of reminiscences by Charles Friend's daughter, Jane, Jennie Stephenson. I wondered if she might have mentioned something about M.W. Cumbea. Unfortunately, she did not mention Major. There were numerous interesting notes, which I can only touch upon here. For one thing, I learned that White Hill

was Friend's summer home. He lived, for the most part, in a house in Petersburg. The plantation was ruined by Union occupation during the siege of Petersburg. The Friend family returned to White Hill after the war, mainly because they could no longer afford the home in Petersburg, and they found the place almost unrecognizable. They eked out a marginal existence by subsistence farming. The woods had been cut down for the use of the armies, and the contents of the home had disappeared. There was looting on the part of the newly freed slaves, who allegedly were joined by the overseer, not Major of course. Only a few of the oldest and most reliable of the former slaves stayed on the plantation. In regard to the slaves, Jennie S. remembered that slave marriages (and funerals), prior to the war, were big events on the plantation. The grooms- to- be had to ask the master, Charles, for permission to marry. In Jennie's memory, all the slaves were either married couples or children. Couples had their "own" small dwellings with gardens and a pig. She remembered the Rev. Gibson who Charles mentioned in his Diary. I mention the slave marriages because one often reads in so called histories that slaves were not permitted to marry. This really was an option of the master, who could permit or encourage slave marriages that would have religious or moral status but no civil status. Mrs. Friend used to have the slave children at the big house for religious instruction, and she would reward quick learning and smart answers with sweets. I could go on, but instead I will go on to bed. The Park Service has White Hill photos which are in the public domain, which I can use in the family history without getting permission.
Best wishes,
Sam

A continuation of the above message:

I thought it worth mentioning that, after the war, there were unburied and partially buried bodies all over the former White Hill plantation. The federal government offered five dollars for every skeleton that included a skull. The Friend family and their neighbors partly supported themselves by selling skulls to the feds. Many of those skulls ended up in the federal cemetery in City Point, now Hopewell.

Prince George Chancery Orders and Decrees, Major W. Cumbea is mentioned on pp. 120, 158, 187, 219, and 309.

From **Fiduciary Bonds 1865-1891**, 1872, Bond A, p. 94- J. Wesley Friend on Sept. 12, 1872 was bound in the sum of $ 500 as administrator of M. W. Cumbea, deceased.

I checked the **Index to Marriages**, females, and found no Cumbeas. Under Males, I found the marriage of Willard Glover Cumbea to Mary Shaw Hatch on Jan. 18, 1898, in Book 1, p. 74.

Prince George County Deed Book 29 has references to Major and Adelia on pp. 343, 344, and 605. Page 605 gives the location of Major's farm.

Deed Book 29, p. 343 reads in part: Cumbea & Wife Against SoSide RR Co-Petersburg, VA, Jan. 27th, 1870, Gen. Wm. Mahone, Prst., [il. word] I propose to grant to the Southside RailRoad Company, for the sum of five hundred dollars, one half to be paid in cash, and the remainder in two equal payments in three and six months, the privilege of going upon my land, at such point or points as they may see fit, between their RailRoad track and the Appomattox River.... Agreement was reached and signed. The whole document and both signatures, M.W. Cumbea and Adelia M.Cumbea, seem to be in the same handwriting.

p. 605, A.M. Cumbea and children, Homestead Deed: the property was bounded on the East by the land of John Hare, West by the Corporation line of the City of Petersburg, South the land of O.P. Hare, and North by the Appomattox River. If the limits of Petersburg were the same in 1870 as they are now- and I plan to check on this-the farm would have been across the river from South Park Mall, but downstream from the Mall, about where the Vulcan gravel company is now. I plan to check with Vulcan about any possible cemeteries on their property.

Deed Book 31, p. 675 says that the plat for part of the Cumbea farm can be found on p. 240 in Plat Book [# , ? , piece of tape over it!].

The estate was described thusly: land worth $1700, two mules at $100, 1 cooking stove and necessary cooking utensils worth $10, 2 bedsteads with bedding worth $12, 1 Bureau worth $4, 6 chairs worth $2, 1 table worth $2, 2 plows worth $3, 1 wagon worth $12, 1 axe worth $1, and 1 wheat cradle worth $2.

Deed Book 42, p. 576 records the sale of 31 acres by Semalina C. Spivey to W.G. Cumbea. Page 565 has the signature of Mollie S. Cumbea, which looks for all the world for once the real thing.

Deed Book 43, p. 497, records the inheritance of about 700 acres of land by three survivors of George Hatch, one of whom was Mary Hatch Cumbea. I only glanced at this, will read it more closely later.

From an email sent on May 27, 2004:

" This morning I took some more notes at the Prince George Count Court House.

From **Deed Book 29, p. 605**:[with spelling, punctuation, etc. as I found it]
Whereas, M.W. Cumbea, late of the County of Prince George in the State of Virginia, departed this life on the 10th of May 1872, leaving surviving him. his wife Adelia M. Cumbea and two children , James Edward and W.G.[the G is illegible] Cumbea infants under the age of twenty-one years, without having claimed or set aside a Homestead. And whereas the said Adelia M.Cumbea, relect of the said M.W. Cumbea, dec'd, is desirous to claim and set aside for herself and her children out of the property whereof her late husband died seized and possessed a homestead of the value of two thousand dollars as provided for by the Constitution of the State of Virginia and an act of the Legislature of the said State passed in pursuance thereby and approved on the 27th day of June 1870, commonly known as the "Homestead Act." Nowtherefore this deed made this 5th day of August 1873, witnesseth, that the said Adelia M. Cumbea for the benefit of herself and her children doth claim and set aside as her homestead the following property-towit: all that tract or parcel of land lying and situate in the County of Prince George containing fifty-eight acres and boundeth as follows: East by the land of John Hare; West by the Corporative line of the City of Petersburg; South by the land of O.P. Hare; and

North by the Appomattox River; it being in all respects the same land whereof the late M.W. Cumbea died, seized and whereon he resided at the time of his death and being of the value of $1700.00. Two mules @$50 $100 1 cooking stove and necessary cooking utensils $10.00 2 Bedsteads and bedding 12.00 1 Bureau 4.00 6 chairs 2.00 1 table 2.00 2 plows $3.00 1 wagon 12.00 1 axe 1.00 1 wheat cradle 2.00 making a total valuation of eighteen hundred and forty-eight dollars.

The above includes what purports to be Adelia Cumbea's signature. The writing looks a little different but suspiciously similar to the writing of the clerk who made the entry. In earlier entries, the writing of M.W. and Adelia Cumbea seems identical.

The date on this entry is interesting, for it is near the time when Adelia Cumbea died. I don't recall the exact date - and will try to look it up- but she lived only about a year after Major.

Book 31, p. 675:
E.M. Cox purchased property of the estate of M.W.Cumbea, which had been ordered sold by Rich'd Davis: 3.09 acres, bought for $155.

Book 43, p. 497:
This deals with the disposition of the estate of George Hatch. His estate included two tracts of land, one of 576 and 3/4 acres and the other of 202 acres. Mary Hatch Cumbea's brothers got the larger tract, and she inherited 202 acres. This includes the signature of Mary Cumbea."

An email sent on May 28, 2004:

"It is very interesting to me too. Mrs. Major W. before now has seemed to

have been perhaps a weak figure, mainly because she died rather young
and so soon after the death of her husband. It looks now, however, like
she was a person with some foresight and willingness to assert herself.
Her death record did not identify the cause of death, and I would be
very interested to know what happened. I wonder if her health was poor
along and she was trying to protect her children by keeping the
property. But the property seemed to have gone to a John Cumbea after
the death of Adelia, probably because he was Major's oldest surviving
child. She evidently died intestate. The suit that I wrote about some
months ago was Cumbea vs. Cumbea, i.e., the sons of Major and Adelia vs.
John Cumbea. It took about ten years to settle that suit, and by the
time it was settled, there was very little left for Willard and Jim.

The part about Mary Cumbea inheriting 202 acres of land is also
revealing. I had sort of assumed that orphan Willard never got a break,
but it looks like his wife inherited a substantial inheritance.

Changing the subject for a moment, I learned something a couple of weeks
ago about the date of the marriage of Major W. "Cumby" and Nancy B.

Morgan. The date you will see in various transcriptions as the date of

the marriage is really the date that the minister turned in his return,

the date the marriage was officially noted, not the date it was performed. I don't have the notes in front of me now, but the minister

wrote something very similar to " to the best of my recollection [!],

these are the people I have married since my last report", with Major

Cumby and Nancy B. Morgan listed.

My 7 year old will be out of school in a few days, and, because I am not

sending him to day care this summer but having him with me during the

day, my time for research will disappear for about three months. It may

be a while before anything new comes from me. Once there is time, I hope

to trace the deed and find exactly where the Cumbeas lived. Given that

it seems to be within present day Petersburg, there is some remote

chance that the actual house that they lived in might still be standing.

Wouldn't it be a thrill to find that!

Sam"

----- Original Message -----
From: Steve <ᵗ> Cumbea
To: Sam Whitby <mailto:sam.whitby@verizon.net>
Sent: Friday, May 28, 2004 8:07 AM

Subject: RE: family

Sam: This is really good stuff. Thanks so much for finding and forwarding.

Order Book 1871-75, p. 147, mentions Mary Cumbia, widow of M.W. Cumbia.

The Prince George Birth Register listed the birth of Harriett G. Cumbea on July 25, 1871.

An email from Susan Lloyd, Feb.16, 2004:

" DESCENDANTS OF JAMES EDWARD CUMBEA
>
> 1. James Edward Cumbea Born: August 6, 1862 in Petersurg, Virginia.
Died:
> May 20, 1949 in Atlanta, Georgia. Burial: May 22, 1949 in Oakland
Cemetery,
> Atlanta. Georgia.
>   + Lula Josephine Harville Born: November 14, 1868 in Atlanta, Georgia.
> Died: August 20, 1970 in Atlanta, Georgia. Married: September 15, 1886.
>   2. Mabel Lanier Cumbea Born: June 26, 1888 in Atlanta, Georgia.
> Died: August 7, 1970 in Atlanta, Georgia
>   + Olin Mason Stanton, Sr. Born: September 30, 1886 in Winder,
> Georgia. Died: October 16, 1957 in Atlanta, Georgia. The are both buried in
> Westview Cemetery in Atlanta.
>   3. Baby Girl Stanton Born: 1910 in Atlanta, Georgia Died: 1910
> in Atlanta, Georgia.
>   3. Baby Boy Stanton Born: 1911 in Oklahoma Died: 1911

in
> Oklahoma.
>   3. Baby Girl Stanton Born: 1911 in Oklahoma Died: 1911
in
> Okalahoma
>   3. Mabel Cumbea Stanton Born: June 11, 1912 in Dallas,
Texas
> Died: December 10, 1997 in Kennesaw, Georgia
>   + Howard Jack Barker Born: July 25, 1911 in Rochester,
New
> York Died: July 1, 1992 in Atlanta, Georgia. Married August 19,
1933 in
> Center, Alabama.
>   3. Jeanne Oline Stanton Born: May 9, 1916 in Omaha,
Nebraska.
>   + Berry Lee Whaley, Sr. Born: February 13, 1904 un
Atlanta,
> Georgia Died: February 3, 1999 in Atlanta, Georgia   Married July
26,
1941 in
> Atlanta, Georgia Burial: February 6, 1999 Arlington Memorial
Park, Sandy
> Springs, Georgia.
>   4. Barry Lee Whaley, Jr.   Born: January 3, 1948 in Atlanta,
> Georgia
>   + Dorothy Faye Branam Born: October 25, 1950 in
> Gatlinburg, Tennessee Married: December 19, 1980 in Decatur,
Georgia.
>   4 Jeanne Oline Whaley Born: January 3, 1948 in Atlanta,
> Georgia
>   + Dennis Alexander LaRosa Born: September 25, 1947
in
> Brooklyn, New York Married: October 21, 1968
>   5 Gina Leigh LaRosa Born: December 12, 1969 in
Atlanta,
> Georgia
>   + Paul Alan Sabin Born: May 2, 1967 in Cleveland,
> Ohio Married: June 22, 1991 in Marietta, Georgia
>   6 Samantha Britain Sabin Born: January 7, 1993.
>   6 Bradley Elizabeth Sabin Born: May 18 1995.

```
>                  5  Donna Marie LaRosa  Born:  October 3, 1976
>                     + Garrett Douglas Sever   Married August 29, 1998 in
> Roswell, Georgia.
>                     6 Gabriel Tate Sever   Born: November 21, 2002 in
> Germany
>                     6 Brenna Lenore Sever  Born: November 21, 2002 in
> Germany
>               *2nd Husband of Jeanne Oline Whaley:
>                  + Michael Earl Hopper   Born: January 25, 1947 in
> Alabama   Married  August 27, 1987 in Roswell, Georgia.
>               *3rd Husband of Jeanne Oline Whaley:
>                  + Robert Tate Litteer   Born May 15, 1942 in
Atlanta,
> Georgia.
>        3,  Olin Mason Stanton, Jr.   Born July 3, 1918 in Decatur,
Georgia
> Died:  July 26, 1983 in Williston, Levy County, Florida   Burial:
July
28,
> 1983.  (Orange Hill Cemetery)
>           + Emmie Evelyn Harper   Born:  October 4, 1911 in Griffin,
> Georgia   Died:  May 9, 1968, Griffin, Georgia   Married:
December 1,
1946 in
> Atlanta, Georgia  Burial:  May 11, 1968 Atlanta, Fulton County,
Georgia
(Westview
> Cemetery)
>         4  Susan Gayle Stanton   Born:  June 3, 1949
>             + Martin Franklin Walker, Jr.   Born January 22, 1945
> Married  June 24, 1967 in Atlanta, Georgia .
>                  5 Martin Stanton Walker   Born: November 25, 1969 in
> Austell, Georgia.
>                  + Terisa Ann Cerniglia  Born:  May 15, 1971 in
Atlanta,
> Georgia.  Married:  January 28, 1993 in Jonesboro, Georgia.
>                     6 Jessica Lynn Walker   Born September 27, 1993 in
> Atlanta, Georgia.
>                     6 Scott Stanton Walker   Born:  June 10, 1998 in
> Atlanta, Georgia
```

>   5 Charles Scott Walker   Born: June 16, 1971 in Austell,
> Georgia   Died: February 1, 1991 in Al Saban, Saudi Arabia.
>   5 Baby Walker   Born: January 3, 1975 in Austell,
Georgia.
> Died: January 3, 1975,
>   5 Christopher Daniel Walker   Born: January 27, 1976 in
> Austell, Georgia.
>   + Christina Marie Catherine Albert   Born: April
30.1976
> in Lima, Ohio   Married   May 2, 1998 in Hampton, Georgia
>   6 Alexandria Skye Walker   Born: January 5, 2000 in
> Riverdale, Clayton County, Georgia.
>   *2nd Husband of Susan Gayle Stanton:
>   + Ronald Allen Lloyd   Born: October 5, 1952 in
Phoenix,
> Arizona   Married April 5, 1985 in Jonesboro, Georgia
>   *2nd Wife of Olin Mason Stanton, Jr.
>   + Rheba Tipton Yound   Born: June 12, 1910 in North
Carolina
> Died: 1983 in Williston, Florida   Married June 13, 1970 in Boone,
North
> Carolina.   Buriel: Willison, Levy County, Florida (Orange Hill
Cemetery)
>
> 2   Willard Earl Cumbea   Born: July 22, 1890 in Atlanta, Georgia
Died:
> December 27, 1953 in Atlanta, Fulton County, Georgia   Burial:
December
29,
> 1953, Atlanta, Fulton County, Georgia (Oakland Cemetery)
>
>
> Finally,   Sorry it has taken me so long to get this to you.   I can't wait
to
> see all that you have come up with in the family tree.   I want you to
know
how
> happy and proud I am of you for all your many, many long days of
work on
our

> tree. We are all very proud of you and I'm sure all of our ancestors are,
too!
>
> Love and appreciation,
> Susan"

The **Prince George Death Register** listed the death of M.W.Cumbea on May 10, 1872. It gave as his parents "Thos & Agnes Cumbea."

The **Bureau of Vital Statistics** verified the above information regarding the death of Major, and it also reported the death of A. [Adelia] M. [Mary] Cumbea. She died at 37 of unknown causes on Nov. 9, 1873. Her parents were identified as Wm. C. and Sarah Hobbs. The provider of the information was not identified.

July 9, 1869, William A. Cumbia died in Prince George County, VA, cause unknown, parents were – and Nancy B. Cumbia. He was born in Prince George, unmarried. [He was the son of Major Weatherford Cumbia and Nancy B. Morgan Cumbia. The **Blandford Cemetery records** indicated that the cause of death was consumption.] Nancy Cumbia and David Cumbia are also buried with William. The relationship of David Cumbia is unknown, but a good guess is that he was one of the children of Major and Nancy.

An email sent to interested family members:
"This morning, happening to be in the neighborhood, I stopped by the office of the Blandford Cemetery [in Petersburg, VA]. The secretary let me look at SOME records, and I took notes. My plan was to look at Hobbs plots, to see if Major and Adelia might have been put to rest in one of them, but the secretary could not be

persuaded that there was any such possibility, so I had to be satisfied with what follows:

David Cumby died in Chesterfield on December 13, 1864. The cause of death was diarrhea. My guess is that he was a child of Major and Adelia, but the cemetery records do not indicate the names of the parents. He was born in Chesterfield County. I have not found Cumbys living in Chesterfield County, but maybe this just means that I need to look again.

William A. Cumbia, 21, died on August 1, 1869, from consumption. He was a son of [Major and] Nancy. He was a Civil War vet.

Nancy B. Cumba died on March 1, 1861, from apoplexy, at age 50. Her parents were Jesse and Mary Morgan. Nancy was Major Weatherford's first wife.

A. L. Cumby died on Feb. 21, 1896, at the age of 21 days. This was a child of T.J.Cumby (Thomas Jefferson [should read "Jonathon"], a son of John Henry and Winnifred) and Virginia.

John Henry's daughters, Harriet Early and Emma, are also buried at Blandford."

An email from Larry Mills-

" Sam,

The oldest[child of Willard and Mary Cumbea] was Genevieve:

My grandmother, Mary Shaw, corresponded with a lady named "Aunt Myra" Hobbs

who lived in New Harmony, Indiana. I always thought she was a relative of
Mary Shaw, but now that we know who Adeila Hobbs was, I suspect that she was
related to Willard. Anyway, this lady offered to send Genevieve to high
school if Mary Shaw, who was a widow by then, would send her back to Indiana
to help Myra with her two boys. And that is how Genevieve came to be
educated. By the way, this
Myra Hobbs was something of a pioneer. She became a licensed chiropractor
in Indiana before it was fashionable for women to do such things.
Genevieve died in her sleep at age 22 of an unknown cause.

Next, is Lina Evangaline:

After many years of living and working on a farm in Laclede County she and
her husband, Virgil Degraffenreid, moved to town opened a hotel and
restaurant, and became successful entrepreneurs Here in 2003 Lina is 92
years old and still a very much "take charge" person.

The baby of the family was Arlene Virginia. In 2003 she is 86 years old and
still lives alone in her own apartment. During World War II she was a
prototypical "Rosie the Riviter". She worked at the Ford plant in Kansas
City where they made airplane engines. She was an inspector checking the

tolerances of engine parts with gauges.

Hope this is helpful, Larry"

Lina Evangeline died in 2005.

Another email, sent by Sam Whitby to Cumbia Cousins:

"My son David and I found [at the LVA] [**city directory**] records indicating that a John
R.Cumbea lived in Richmond in the late 1800s and early 1900s. That
finding was exciting, for Major Weatherford Cumbia/Cumbea had a son
named John R., and we hoped that we had found a branch of Major's line
which still lived in the Richmond area. This morning we returned to the
LVA to look at some different records. Our findings cast some doubt upon
our interpretation.

We looked at **Bureau of Vital Statistics, Old Birth Index,** Reels 1 and 9.
In Reel 1 I found the birth of John R. Cumbee in Halifax County on March
10, 1857. His parents were A. and L. J. Cumbee. Another record
indicated that William B. Cumbee was born to Alexander and Lou Cumbee,
which gives us the names indicated earlier by only initials.

My guess,
which is little more than that yet, is that the John R. in Richmond was
the one born in Halifax County. I think that Major's son would have
probably been too old to have still been working as a machinist in 1912.
The Halifax John R. would not exactly have been young then, but he might
still have been working. More evidence will be needed before we can know
for sure. To further complicate matters, James L. and Emily also had a son named John R."

Reel 9 recorded the birth of Pearl Cumbea in Richmond, VA, on Feb. 2,
1874, and her parents were Jno. and Kate C. Cumbea (p. 313 of
register). Mary A. Cumber was born on Jan. 15, 1878 to John R. and C.C.
Cumber (p. 510 of the register). I checked the actual register and
found that the name was very faded and probably should have been
transcribed as Cumbea.

Reel 9 also recorded the birth on Dec. 1, 1868, of male twins to M.W.
and Adelia M. G. Cumbia. Unfortunately, no names were given for the
still mysterious twins. Harriet G. Cumbia was born to Major and Adelia
Cumbia on July 25, 1871. Susan and Steve, what do you make of this?

David very laboriously read the **1850 Census of Campbell County**. He found
on p.203, Leesville, the family of Simeon Comby, 47; Aimy , 50; Mary,
25; Thomas, 23; Martha, 21; Sarah, 19; William, 16; Narcissus, 13. I
think that Simeon was the same person of that name who lived in
Appomattox County later in the 1880s."

John R. Cumbea, shows on the **Richmond City Directories** of 1898, 1900, and 1901. He also appears in 1912, probably on the intervening editions also, but they were not checked. John J. Cumbea appears on the 1893-4 and 1895-6 editions, and this seems to have really been John R. I think this John Cumby may have been the son of Major and Nancy. In 1901 there was also a Miss Mamie Cumbea, asst bkkpr, W.D. Moses. There was also a Maxwell Combe, shoemaker.

John R. Cumbea died on April 19, 1922, at 85, from myocarditis. The death certificate # is 627-8656, and it does not identify his mother, gives John R. Cumbea as his father [does not seem right]. JRC is buried in Oakwood Cemetery (old). Capt Thos Cunningham provided the info.

The **Petersburg City Directory of 1897** shows John Henry Cumbia's children Annie B., H. Early,Viola, and Thomas J., living in Petersburg. The daughters were mill hands, and T.J. was a trunkmaker.

Deaths – Reel 6, LVA –
David Lee Cumbia, Death Certificate 559-303,
Florence A. Cumbia,   "   501-23707.

Register of Deaths, Prince George County-found at Prince George County Courthouse-
Line 561 – Cumbia, M.W., WM, farmer, died May 10, 1872, due to meningitus, born in Charlotte County, parents were Thos. & Agnes Cumbia, wife was Adelia M. Cumbia.

William A. Cumbia, died on July 9, 1869, in Prince George County, cause unknown [elsewhere, I have seen the cause given as consumption], born in Prince George Co., unmarried, parents were – and Nancy B. Cumbia.

Register of Births, Prince George County-Courthouse-
Line 976-July 25, 1871, Harriett G. Cumbea was born, parents were M.W. Cumbea, farmer, and A.M.G. Cumbea, in Bland Township. [Steve Cumbea reported to me by email that the tombstone of Willard Glover Cumbea gives July 25, 1871 as his birthdate. The reason for this discrepancy is presently unknown.]

Prince George County Birth Register-
1857-records the birth of a male slave named Washington, who belonged to Major Cumbia [perhaps Cumbie], did not give the names of the parents.

Marriage Register-
Willard Glover Cumbea, machinist, who was born in Petersburg, married Mary Shaw on January 18, 1898. His parents were Major Weatherford Cumbea and Delia M. Cumbea. John T. Moore performed the ceremony.

Prince George Chancery Orders and Decrees, at the Prince George County Courthouse- Cumbea records are found on pp. 120, 158,187,219,309.

P.120- " Robert Gilliam appointed guardian ...to defend the infant defendants in their cause" Cumbea vs. Cumbea & als- " land cannot be conveniently divided in kind among the parties entitled thereto, the court doth adjudge, order and decree, that Rich'd B. Davis, who is hereby appointed a special [looks like counselor] for the purposes, proceed to sell the said tract of land...."

John R. Cumbea, evidently Major's son, had purchased ~50 acres of Major's land, which was ordered sold to pay Major's debts and to support his orphaned children, Willard Glover Cumbea and James Edward Cumbea.

P. 309- J. Wesley Friend , guardian, to receive $ 54 for the maintenance and support of James Edward and Willard Glover Cumbea at the asylum in Richmond whither they have been sent.

Charlotte County, Virginia-

The notes that follow, on Charlotte County, were made from microfilm copies at the LVA

Charlotte County Deed Book 11, p. 225-
" Received this 5th of November 1809 the sum of one hundred pounds six shillings of Major Cumbee for the purchase of a Negro woman and child, the woman named Hannah and the child called Harriot delivered unto the possession on yesterday at Charlotte Court House a good & absolute title to the said slaves to the said Cumbee."

Charlotte Deed Book 8, p. 263-
Wiliam Allin Sublett sold Thomas Cumbee 148 acres for 15 pounds.[This William Sublett may be Agnes Weatherford's grandfather, her mother's father.]

Charlotte Deed Book 9, p. 117-
Thomas Cumby sold the above land for 80 pounds, his mark.

Charlotte Deed Book 9, p. 158-
In a reference to the above sale: "Susannah Cumbee the wife of this Thomas Cumbee"

Deed Book 14, p. 130- microfilm copy is unreadable.

Deed Book 14, p. 149 – illegible, refers to Major Cumbee
Maggie his wife- when this note was originally taken, wife's name was unclear, noted as Aggy, Bggy, or Maggy.

Charlotte Co. Marriage Register, No.1, 1782-1853-LVA
microfilm
M. Cumby, p.32, Dec. 26, 1804, Major Cumbee md. Margaret Mical, married by Jno Chappell,

Harrison Cumbee md. Eliza Earle in 1825[il.],
Daniel Cumby md. – Carwiles on June 4, 1823,
Elizabeth Cumby md. William Rutledge on May 5, 1828,
Patsy Cumbee md. Elijah South on March 27, 1805,

Register # 2-
J.H.Combey md. Sarah Blankenship on Dec. 29, 1856, son of
Tho. T. and Eliz. Combey, bride and groom were born in
Campbell Co.

In 1769 William Black sued Thomas Cumbo, Sr. Thomas
Cumbo was among [those] "...ordered [to] forthwith clear
and keep the said road [from the courthouse to Milner's
Ordinary] in repair."

Order references are as follows: ...[to be filled in later].

Some Charlotte County, VA, marriages:

Agness Weatherford married James Harper on December 26,
1782. She was an aunt of Thomas Cumby's wife.

Major Cumbee married Margaret Mical [not McMichael]on
Dec. 22, 1804. He was a son of Thomas Cumby (Sr.).

Maria Cumbee married Andrew Young on Jan. 7, 1828. She
was a daughter of Charles Cumbee.

Elizabeth Cumbee married Robert Ales on Oct. 31, 1836. She
was a daughter of Morgan Cumbee.

Elizabeth Cumby married William Rutledge on May 5, 1828.
She was married by Daniel Petty, the minister who married
Major and Nancy Morgan. She was a daughter of Charles
Cumby.

Daniel Cumbee married Mary Carwiles on June 14, 1822. He later was widowed, married a woman named Nancy, and started a line with a son named General Lee Cumbey in Giles Co. My fallible memory says that Daniel was a son of the elder Major Cumbee of Charlotte Co.

Harrison Cumbee married Eliza East on Oct. 2, 1826.

Simeon Cumby married Amy Loggins on Nov. 16, 1818. Simeon lived later in Campbell, then Appomattox.

Thomas Cumby married Dicy Loggins [love that name] on Nov.27, 1823.

Thomas Cumby married Eliza Smith on April 6, 1829. He was a widower, lived later in Campbell Co., moved to Appomattox Co., and started a line there.

**GILES COUNTY VIRGINIA
HISTORY – FAMILIES By
RESEARCH COMMITTEE GILES CO. HISTORICAL
SOCIETY – has many references to people named
Cumbee, Cumby, Cumbey, and Cumba.**

1850 Census of Giles County-
Family 69-Major Cumley [probably should be Cumby], 25, chairmaker, was in the household of John Conoway.

Family 772- Mary Cumley, 50, was a pauper [Mrs. Daniel Cumby?].

Family 182- Susan Cumbly, was 26. Ann T. Cumbly was 3.

From *Giles County Virginia, 1860 Census Annotated-*
Family 426-
Thomas Cumbie, 29, farm laborer, VA,
Sarah Cumbie, 22, Ohio,
Margaret Cumbie, 2, VA,
William Cumbie, 6/12, VA,
Thomas md. Sarah Harless on 9 August 1854, Thomas was born in Charlotte County, VA, son of Daniel and Mary Cumbie,

Family 435-Jackson Willams household, dtr., married Thomas A. Cumbee on 23 Dec. 1870.

Family 565-Jackson Cumbie, 22, farm laborer, was in the household of John H. Fillingen, blacksmith.

Family 79-Jane Cumbie, 18, a "pauper," was in the household of John E. Stafford.

Family 362- From notes, Ellen Tawney, 15 in 1860, married General Cumbee 2 June 1862. Pittsylvania County, Virginia- She was Ellen Jane Tawney, and he was a son of Daniel and M[ary].

From **MARRIAGES OF PITTSYLVANIA COUNTY** –
Nov. 27, 1820- John McDowell married Eunice Weatherford, Sur. Thomas Cumley [this almost certainly should be Cumby] and John Weatherford, father of Eunice and Eunice herself signed the certificate, p. 71. According to several researchers, Agnes died in about 1830, and her last child was raised by the McDowells. I have no evidence regarding this claim, and I think rather that it is likely mistaken.

I found the Consent for the marriage of John McDowell and Eunice Weatherford. John Weatherford's signature and Eunice's signature were on it. John's signature and what purports to be Thomas Cummbe's signature are also on the document, with both signatures in the same distinctive handwriting. Thomas could not read or write, so someone evidently signed for him.

The Marriage Register and the Consent indicate that Thomas Cumby was surety for the above marriage.

"John Weatherford Remembered as Unstoppable Dissenting Preacher" is at http://www.victorianvilla.com/sims-mitchell/local/articles/phsp/005/ . It tells the story of Weatherford's imprisonment at the Chesterfield County jail, including the memory of Weatherford's martyr scars on his hands.

From **PITTSYLVANIA COUNTY. VIRGINIA CEMETERY RECORDS, VOL. 1**, p. 109- found at the Library of Virginia-
"Off Rt. 640 just south of Rt. 832 turn west of Shockoe Baptist Church turnoff and continue on road to end. In the middle of a cultivated field under a walnut tree is a tombstone for 'Elder John Weatherford b. 1740 d. Jan. 23, 1833'… other graves…rocks…."

I have visited the gravesite of John Weatherford. Note that there are two Shockoe Baptist Churches, one black and one white. Both are old, and both have rather large and old cemeteries. When you are on Rt. 832 and headed away from Chatham, you must turn right onto 640 in order to go to the "white" church. If in doubt, you may recognize it by its being the one with a large historical marker about the grave of John Weatherford. A cemetery is at the church, but Rev. Weatherford is not buried there. A dirt road goes off of 640 beside the church. You take the dirt road a few hundred yards past the church, beyond an old cabin. The road will bear to the left and cross a field. The cemetery is in the field. Many small trees have grown up in the cemetery. A couple of larger trees are near the center of the cemetery. To the best that I could tell, only one grave had a marker other than a field stone. That marker had the initials J and W on it, with another badly eroded initial between them.

For more about John Weatherford, see *HISTORY OF THE RISE AND PROGRESS OF THE BAPTISTS IN VIRGINIA*, by Semple. John Weatherford succeeded John Kerr, Sr., as pastor of County Line Baptist Church. John Kerr's son, John Kerr, LLD, of NC had Kerr Dam named after him.

An interesting site on Weatherford genealogy is at http://freepages.genealogy.rootsweb.com~weatherford/ .

The web page of the Chesterfield jail contends that Weatherford was jailed for not seeking a license as a Presbyterian. The web page is at http://chesterfield.gov/ConstitutionalOfficers/Sheriff/History.asp .

FAMILY GENEALOGY RESOURCES INDEX, at LVA-

Mentions Cumbee and Cumbo family files at Wytheville Community College, Kegley Library. It also mentions a Cumbow family file at the Historical Society of Washington Community College, Abingdon, VA. I have not checked either file and do not know whether or not they contain information useful to Cumbia researchers.

THE ROSTER OF UNION SOLDIERS 1861-1865, at the Library of Virgina-
p. 250, reference to John Cumby, US Col'd Cavalry;
p. 224, reference to Combe, 2nd Col'd Infantry;
page was not noted, but John G. and James Cumbo from NC served in the Union Army.

1860 Census of Wise County, Texas-

Edward Cumby-	42-Farmer-b. VA- may be a brother of George	
Lucinda " -	33- b. S.Carolina	
Odesca A. " -	16- b. Tennessee	
William W. " -	14- "	
Caroline Horne -	22- b. Missouri	
William "	8/12- b. Arkansas	

An email sent on July 7, 2003:

"Last week, while I was waiting at the LVA for them to pull some documents that I wanted to see, I checked out some census indexes other than Virginia's. George and Major had at least three brothers about whom we know nothing. My guess is that that they moved out of state.

For what it is worth, I found the following:

1850 Census of Tennessee, Vol. 2

Cumby, Edward, 30, b. in VA; Lucinda, 25, b. in SC; Loduskia A., 6; William W., 4. I also found Combey, Richard, 30, b. in VA; Nancy, 28, b. in VA; James H., 19; Elizabeth, 25; William Y., 6; Mary C., 3; Martha F., 2; and John, 1.

I know from earlier research that Edward's family was living in Texas by 1860. I am not sure, but I "seem" to remember Richard's family being in Texas also. There was also a Robert Cumby in Texas, born in Virginia. My gut feeling at this time, little more than a strong hunch, is that Thomas and Agnes's other three sons moved out of state after her death and that they are some or all of the above- Edward, Richard, and Robert. Anybody have any connections in Texas that can be persuaded to follow up on this hunch?"

An email from Gloria Cumbia Pulliam, Feb. 9, 2004:
Ruth Carolyn Cumbia Snead is buried at Clover Cemetery (Date of Death 11-25-01)
David Ray Pulliam is buried at Buffalo Baptist Church Cemetery (Date of Death 9-9-01
Mama's date of death was 9-1-01
Hope this will help - if you need any other info - I will try!
Have a great day!

Paul Heinegg has a web page at
http://www.freeafricanamericans.com/Virginia_NC.htm .

From **VIRGINIA MAGAZINE OF HISTORY AND BIOGRAPHY (VMHB), Vol. VII, p. 232-**

"To the Honorable Sir Wm. Berkeley Knight Governor & c. And the Honorable Council of Virginia
The humble petition of Wm. Whittacre
Sheweth
That he formerly bought of Mr. Thomas Bushrod a Mulatta named Manuel who bought him of Colo. Wm. Smith's Assignee as a Slave for Ever but in September 1644 the said Servant was by the Assembly judged no Slave but to serve as other Christian servants do and was freed in September 1665."
Wm. Whittacre was a member of the House of Burgesses

From **VIRGINIA COLONIAL ABSTRACTS, Ser. 2, Vol. 4, p. 48-**

"To all & whereas & Now know yee that I ye said Sr. Wm. Berkeley, etc., give and grant unto Emannel Cambew Negro 50 acres of Land according to the ancient Lawful bounds thereof, scituate in James Citty County, the said Land being part of a greater Quantity formerly granted unto Will Davis and Lately found to be in Escheate, 18 April 1667."

I have seen the above land patent on microfilm at the Library of Virginia. The handwriting is small and hard to read, but it is apparent that "Cambew" could just as easily be read as "Camboo" or "Comboo."

From **JAMES CITY COUNTY, VA, LAND TAX RECORDS, 1782-1813-**

Sarah Cumbo taxed on 53 acres of land from 1800 through 1812, perhaps more, not all were checked. William Farthing, deceased , or rather, his estate, was taxed on 125 acres.

From *BRUTON AND MIDDLETON PARISHES REGISTER JAMES CITY COUNTY, VIRGINIA , 1662-1797, by Chappelear-*

pp. 35, 36-

1786- James Johnson Cumbo, son of Solomon & -- b. May;

1787-Elizabeth Cumbo daughter of Solomon Cumbo & -- born Nov. 20;

1790- Sarah Cumbo daughter of Solomon Cumbo & -- b. Aug.19.

From *THE VESTRY BOOK AND REGISTER OF ST. PETER'S PARRISH* [New Kent and James City Counties], 1684-1786, transcribed and edited by C. G. Chamberlayne –

1689- -- Cumbo, processioner;

Eliz: daugh t : to Richd Cumbo bapt: 13th day of May 168-;

Mention of Turner Cumbo

VMHB, Vol. 17, p. 400- mentions the Will of Abell Gower, County Gloucester [England], Esquire, 1632, Witnesses include John Combey. Note is from "Virginia Gleanings in England."

VMHB, Vol. 3, p. 280-"Abstracts of Virginia Land Patents" "John Dennett 200 acres in the County of James … due for the transportation of four persons…[one of whom was] Ann Combey. By West, Aug. 19, 1635."

VMHB, Vol. 4, p. 303- from "Shareholders in London Company "-

Thomas Harris sold Thomas Combe one share.

VMHB, Vol. 3, p. 396, from "Instructions from the Lords of His Ma..ties Most Honble Privy Council"

Council includes E. Comby.

From ***CHARLES CITY COUNTY, VIRGINIA – WILLS & DEEDS 1724/5 to 1731***. p.8-
Deed 2, Feb. 1724- Richard Comboo of Westover Parrish, Charles City Co. to Richard Bradford of same, for 5 shillings all land and plantation where he dwells, in Westover Parrish, 100 acres, bounded by Wm. Parrish, Richard Bradford. Signed Richard Comboo

Benjamin Harrison purchased the above land from Bradford.

Paul Heinegg found that in 1758 Richard Cumbo was hauled into court for failing to declare his wife as a titheable. That means that either she was a black or, more likely, the wife of a black. That Richard Cumbo may be Richard, Jr.

From the ***WILLIAM AND MARY QUARTERLY*** (hereafter ***WMQ***), Vol. 9, p. 74-
"Patents Issued During the Regal Government", Book 1, p. 646, William Davis, May 11, 1639, 200 acres,. Adjoining patented land of Alexander Stomar.

VMHB, Vol. 3 (1895), p. 276-
Alexander Stonar [sic], 350 acres lying on a creek next to the Gleab land , and north west upon a creek abutting upon the Otterdams....

From a letter by Cindy Huggett-

"Nathan Edwards

Note Major Weatherford's wife is (1) Elizabeth Edwards and (2) Mary Edwards, daughters of William Edwards and Unknown

Found Nathaniel Edwards of Brunswick Co., VA who married Jane Eaton with children Benjamin Edwards, William Edwards (spouse unknown) and Isaac Edwards.

Jane Eaton is daughter of William Eaton and Mary Rives.

3. John[1] Cumbo, Sr., born say 1702, received a patent on 22 February 1724 for 150 acres in Surry County on both sides of the Rockey Run of Little Creek and the south side of Three Creeks [Patents 12:162]. He was a "Mul°" listed in Col. Nathaniel Harrison's account books which were recorded in the the Surry County estate of his wife Mary Harrison in 1733, and he was listed in the account of sales of the 16 August 1738 Surry County estate of John Barlow [Deeds, Wills 8:318, 881]. He was in Brunswick County, Virginia, in 1738 [Orders 1732-41, 192] and was living in adjoining Northampton County, North Carolina, on 2 July 1746 when a deed mentioned land on Peahill Creek and John Cumbo (on the Brunswick County, Virginia line) [DB 1:260]. On 5 February 1747 **Nathan Edwards** sued him for a 6 pound, 9 shillings debt in Brunswick County claiming that he had absconded. William Petway, who had 30 barrels of Indian corn and part of a crop of tobacco belonging to John Cumbo, paid the debt for him [Brunswick Orders 1743-49, 130]. He was witness to the 20 April 1750 Northampton County deed of John Avent to John Wood for land on Peahill Creek [DB 1:420]. His plantation was probably the Northampton County tract of land called "Cumboes" in the 19 February 1759 Granville will of **William Eaton** [Grimes, *Abstract of N.C. Wills,* 172]. And a 7 August

1761 patent for land in Brunswick County, Virginia, mentions land on the north side of Peahill Creek, up the Stoney Lick Branch, adjacent to Cumboes line [*Magazine of Virginia Genealogy* 33:149 (Patent Book 33:1066)]. James Gowen sued him in Brunswick County court on 27 December 1757 [Orders 1757-9, 143]. He sold 238 acres in Brunswick County on 6 August 1760 [DB 6:595]. On 6 April 1764 he made a Northampton County deed of gift of his cattle and household goods to (his son?) Thomas Cumbo for maintaining him for his lifetime [DB 3:197]. " The material quoted is from Paul Heinegg.

From **Brunswick County, VA, Court Minutes, 1732-1735-**

May Court, 1735, p. 669-On the petition of Francis Elledge against Daniel Cumbe the Sd Elledge not prosecuting it is ordered that the Same be dismist.

P. 307- On the motion of Giddeon Cumbo The Court considering on the motion it is ordered that he be added to the list of Tyths.

p. 373- In an Action of trespass for an Assault[smeared]Robert Cato plt and Thomas Cumbo Deft, the plt not prosecuting it is ordered that the same be dismist.

P. 901-On the presentment of the Grand jury against Thomas Cumbo there being no prosecution it is ordered that the Same be dismist.

From **Deed Book 5**, p. 484-

Joseph Right of Granville Co in North Carolina to John Cumbo Jr of Brunswick Co 30 Dec 1751 14 pounds Va 238 acres which had been a patent to sd ... on South side of Reedy Branch.... Proved 31 Dec 1751.

Deed Book, Volume 3, p. 595 (original)-

John Cumbo of Maherrin Parish in Brunswick Co to Peter Avent of sd Parish. 5 Aug 1760 35 pounds 238 acres which sd John Cumbo bought from Joseph Right & bounded as by the patent to sd Joseph Right 1 Aug 1745. Wit: David Mason, Lewis Sallomon, Lewis Sallomon Jr, William Avent. Proved 26 Jan 1761.

The notes are from *Cavaliers And Pioneers*, by Nell Marion Nugent, *Vol.s 1 and 2*.

From Vol. 1:

p. 285-George Hack, 400 acres. Northhampton Co....1 July 1653....Trans.[portation] of 4 pers[[ons]:..[including] Will Combay...;

p.30 - John Dennett, 200 acres. Co. of James, 10 August 1635. Trans. of 4 pers.: ...Ann Combey;

p.295- Peter Knight, 1200 acres. Northumberland Co. Trans. of 24 persons...[including] Deborah Come.

From Vol. 2-

p. 367 - [From probably 1691] Thomas Franklin, 228 acres. In Lynhaven Par[ish]. Imp[ortation] of 5 pers. Doll & Jane, Indians, Tom, Combo, & Will, Negroes...;

From Vol. 3-

p. 399 - William Colyer... Lapsed L. [lease?]... 150 acres, Surry Co. 1731. Granted John Combow.

In most of the above it is hard to say what, if anything, the data has to do with Cumbia ancestry. The exception is John Combow, for he seems to be the person who made an agreement, a deed of gift, with Thomas Cumbo, Sr., in which Thomas was to support him for the rest of his life. This means it is likely that John was Thomas's father.

I think it is likely that Hack, Dennett, Knight, and Franklin were investors, perhaps sea captains, who received land in exchange for transporting people, probably servants, to the colony of Virginia.

An email sent on 9/23/2004:

"I have been doing some more research on the family tree and history. Later I will send more notes. Now I would like to clarify something that I wrote months ago. I wrote about the Will of William Ludwell Lee. He freed his slaves in his Will, and he tried to make provision for their education. He left part of the Hot Water plantation to be the site of a normal – free – school. Many of his freed slaves stayed at Hot Water, seemingly expecting that they would be educated there. My clarification is that it no longer seems clear or certain that Lee intended precisely that. The free school would more likely have been a free school for white children. Maybe Lee intended blacks there also, but perhaps, probably I would say, not. He did intend for his freed slaves to receive vocational training to prepare them for lives as free workmen. Unfortunately, nothing of the sort seems to have been done, and the normal school itself never happened. Also, another clarification: M. McCartney indicated free black Cumbo's living in the area. I have yet to verify that, although I may later be able to do so. The people who I have found in the area were black and mixed race people called Cumber. There may or may not be a connection. I do not know.

Later, maybe days later, more notes-.

http://bz.llano.net/gowen/melungia/article4.htm mentions that social class was the primary factor in the relationship between John Rolfe and Pocahontas, with Rolfe as commoner and Pocahontas as royalty. The article contains an analysis of race and social class in the 17th century.

http://docsouth.unc.edu/worsham/menu.html is the address of *One of Jackson's Foot Cavalry…*, by John Worsham. The book mentions that John H. Cumbia tore up the battle flag and passed out pieces of it to his comrades, rather than surrender it to northerners. It mentions the death of William "D" Cumbia and his promise to contribute to widows and orphans.

http://www.familysearch.org/ is the address of the Family Search page of the Church of the Latter Day Saints.

I was unable to locate the reference to a Virginian **William Cumby** who moved with his black wife to Texas. My memory is sure on this: that I found the reference. For the time being, I just cannot locate it.

An email from Willie Munn:

Margaret E. Mosley, granddaughter of Edward Green Cumba and Margaret Crowder

(1) Edward Green Cumba b.1842   married   Margaret Crowder b.1850

They had 3 children:

(2) Virginia Eppes Cumba
Martha Roberta Cumba (my grandmother)
Thomas E. Cumba

(2) Virginia Eppes Cumba b.1870   married   Edward Moseley
>   They had 2 children:
>>   (3) **Margaret E. Moseley** b.1890
>>   Lucy Anne Moseley b.1894

Edward Moseley was an old man when he married Virginia Cumba. They had two young daughters when Virginia died. Edward Moseley deserted and his daughters, Margaret and Lucy Anne, were put in an orphanage at Oxford NC.

Lucy Anne at age 14 married her first cousin Herbert Lee Munn and died in 1910 at age 16 of typhoid fever or some similar illness, can't remember just now.

Margaret Moseley, the girl in the picture, was accepted into college and became a school teacher. Only other thing I know about her is that she died in 1924.

Willie Munn
March 14, 2006
The Library of Virginia can be accessed at
http://www.lva.lib.va.us/index.htm . Many, but not all, of the documents can be viewed on the internet.

From an email sent to the Cumbia cousins:

" http://www.freeafricanamericans.com/Cousins_Davenport.htm

Lacking the time to do much research, I have tried in spare

moments to study
the family tree data in order to better understand them. The attached link
is to Paul Heinegg's page. He has added more material on the Cumbo family. I
would encourage you to look at this research and think about it for
yourself. Although I do not necessarily agree with every jot and tittle of
his analysis, he has pointed out some things that are significant, that tend
to support my interpretation of the data. He found Thomas Cumbo, the elder,
on a list of taxables as a Mulatto. Peter Cumbo also was listed as a
Mulatto. That Peter Cumbo married Milly Ramsey in 1785. The Peter who turned
up in my Campbell County research married Nancy Farthing in 1799 or 1800. He
was still living and 100 years old in 1860, so he was probably the same
person who married Milly Ramsey. He and Emmanuel farmed together in Campbell
County. I think it likely that Peter moved with Emmanuel to Campbell County
in order to be counted as white. "Our" Thomas Cumby is not mentioned in
Heinegg's work, but he lived in Halifax, where he married Agnes Weatherford,
Charlotte, where Major Weatherford was born, and in Campbell, where George
A. was born. I think it is likely-no, it is a sure thing- that our Thomas,
Robert Allen's grandfather, knew Thomas Senior, Major Cumbee, Peter and

Emmanuel, and his other relatives in Charlotte/
Halifax/Campbell. He would
no doubt have known that the authorities considered the ethnicity of the
family in deciding what taxes they owed. The sad truth is that in Virginia
in the late 1700s and early 1800s free blacks and mixed race people paid
extra taxes as undesirables. What I am saying is that Robert Allen's
grandfather knew the truth. He died around the time that R.A. was born, and
Robert probably never knew him. Still, maybe, just maybe, Robert Allen knew
the truth. Maybe there you have one source of the family reticence."

An email from Willie Munn, on May 15, 2006:

"Hello Sam,
I called and was able to talk to Mrs. Williams. They had been out of town on vacation for a week.
She doesn't know who the Bible belonged to originally. She mentioned a letter that was in the Bible and still was stunned that they have misplaced copies of everything. She did enter on her genealogy record the following which she read to me on the phone. It is the family of Virginia Eppes Cumba (the young lady in the photo you have) and her husband Edward Lee Mosely. It lists the birthdates of Virginia Anne, Edward Mosely and five children.
Previously I had thought they only had two children before Virginia died in
1899 but that appears to be incorrect.

The children are:

1. Margaret Eppes Mosley b.1892 (She married Bennie Franklin Williams who is the father of Mr. Williams.) Margaret was put in the orphanage by Edward Green and Margaret in 1902 after their mother died in 1899.

2. Robert Graham Mosely b.1889 (This was new information to me.)

3. Lucy Anne Mosely b.1894 (Lucy married Herbert Munn at age 14 and died at age 16 of typhoid fever.) Lucy Anne was put in the orphanage by Edward Green and Margaret in 1902 after their mother died in 1899.

4. John Jackson Mosley b.1896 (This was new information to me.)

5. Bessie Pearl Mosley b.1898 (This was new information to me.)

Don't have any idea who the other three children lived with or what happened to them after their mother died in 1899 and Edward Lee Mosely deserted the family.

Mrs. Williams said she and Bennie will be visiting Mrs. Seaman in June and she will use the opportunity to make more copies of the information and promises to send to me. She did not mention what was in the letter or any additional information which was earlier than Virginia Anne and her family.

I did ask who the Bible belonged to and she said she thought it was Margaret's mother but she couldn't be sure which Margaret. Seems there were too many Margarets in the Cumba line.

Almost forgot. The birthdate for Virginia Anne Cumba is September 30, 1869.
I will have to check to see if Edward Green deserted Sally Tucker in 1868 or 1869.

later,
willie"

An email sent on May 18, 2006:

Img026
This morning I went to the Prince George County Court House and made the attached copy, from Deed Book 31, p.240. At the lower right, unreadable here, are "Map of 63.91 Acres of Land in the County of Prince George and belonging to the Estate of M.W.Cumby Nov. 27, 1874" The original is in color -shaded pencil- and very legible. I apologize for the poor quality of this image made from microfilm, but it was the best that I could do. The area on the right was in brown for arable land, and most of the area on the left was in green, or meadow and adjacent bluffs. The borders of the property are clearly marked, and I would think that a surveryor could find the property. "Condemnation line" appears several places on this plat. Poor Creek runs through the property,as well as the railroad, and the "engine house" is on the left, evidently the railroad engine house. 63.91 acres is different from the 58 acres that I have found in other references to the M.W.Cumbea property. A guess is that the property was newly and more accurately surveyed. The dwelling was probably the family home.

I hope that all of you are well.

Sam

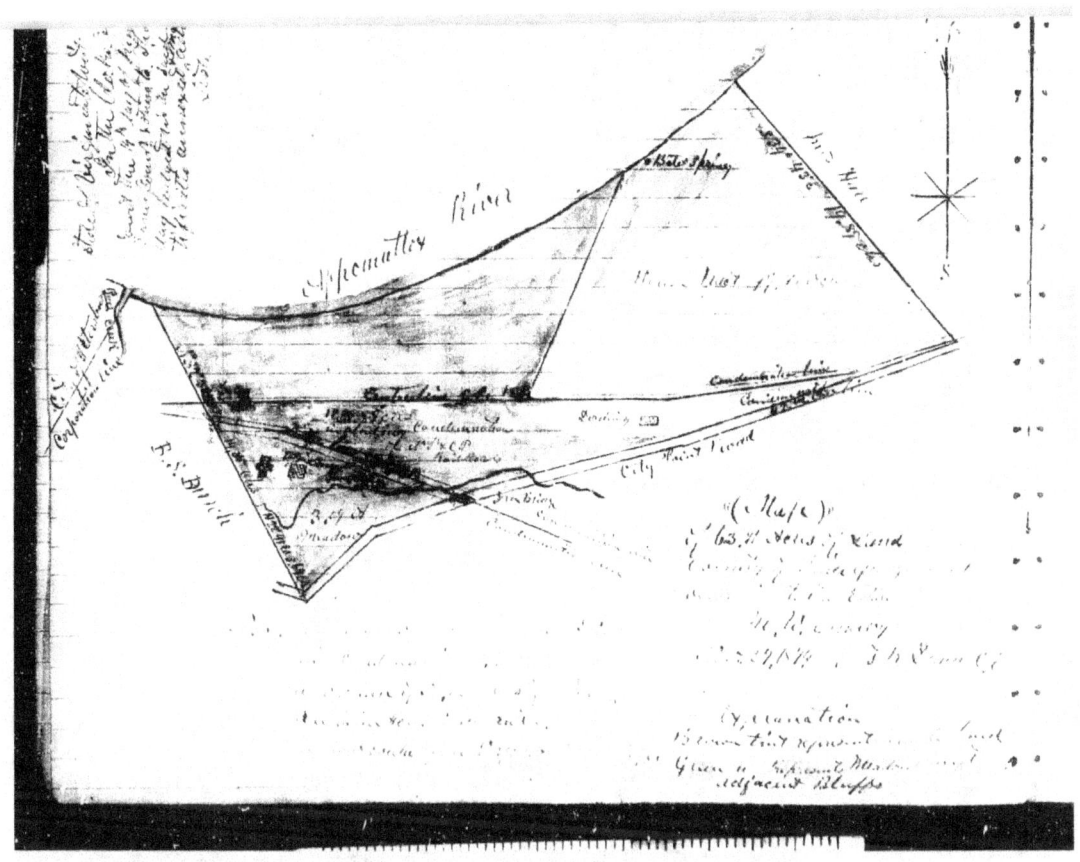

Above is a plat of the farm (Estate) of M.W.Cumby, 1874, found at Prince George Court House, Virginia.

James City County, Keystone of the Commonwealth, by Martha W. McCartney, Copyright by James City County Board of Supervisors, James City County, Virginia, 1997, The Downing Company Publishers- see p. 258; p. 321, which has a map that shows a "Free Negro Settlement Full of Cabins and Paths"; pp. 490-492; p. 478, " In 1667 the General Assembly eliminated baptism as a possible avenue to freedom. This was a departure from the previous consensus that non-Christians' conversion entitled them to their release. By 1670 service for life was the norm for most blacks entering the colony.[By] 1682...all servants from non-Christian countries were considered enslaved."

Dr. William Scarborough wrote *The Overseer: Plantation Management in the Old South*, Baton Rouge, Louisiana State University Press, 1966, mentions M.W.Cumbea on p. 48. A letter from Dr. Scarborough was in the notes shared by Dorothy Cumbea.

The data on Daniel Cumbo was found on Virginia Runaways: Runaway Slave advertisements from 18th century Virginia newspapers, [by]Professor Thomas Costa, University of Virginia's College at Wise, on the internet at
http://etext.lib.virginia.edu/etcbin/ot2www-costa?specfile=/web/data/users/costa/costaslave.o2w&act=surround&offset=889883&tag=Runaway+Slave:+Virginia+Gazette+(Purdie+&+Dixon),+Williamsburg,+September+29,+1768.++&query=Cumbo .

For Combs family genealogy see http://www.combs-families.org/combs/ .

For Josiah Combs' "Combs, a Study in Comparative Philology and Genealogy" go to http://www.combs-families.org/combs/jhc/ms-jhc.html .